HomeBuilders Parenting Series®

Improving Your

Parenting

By Dennis and Barbara Rainey

*"Unless the Lord
builds the house,
its builders
labor in vain"*
(Psalm 127:1a).

FAMILYLIFE™
Bringing Timeless Principles Home
Little Rock, Arkansas

Group
Loveland, Colorado

Group resources actually work!

This Group resource helps you focus on **"The 1 Thing™"**— a life-changing relationship with Jesus Christ. "The 1 Thing" incorporates our **R.E.A.L.** approach to ministry. It reinforces a growing friendship with Jesus, encourages long-term learning, and results in life transformation, because it's:

Relational
Learner-to-learner interaction enhances learning and builds Christian friendships.

Experiential
What learners experience through discussion and action sticks with them up to 9 times longer than what they simply hear or read.

Applicable
The aim of Christian education is to equip learners to be both hearers and doers of God's Word.

Learner-based
Learners understand and retain more when the learning process takes into consideration how they learn best.

Improving Your Parenting

Copyright © 2003 Dennis and Barbara Rainey

Visit our Web site: **www.group.com**

Credits
FamilyLife
Editor: David Boehi

Group Publishing, Inc.
Editor: Matt Lockhart
Chief Creative Officer: Joani Schultz
Copy Editor: Dena Twinem
Art Directors: Jenette L. McEntire, Jean Bruns and Randy Kady
Print Production Artist: Randy Kady
Cover Art Director: Jeff A. Storm
Cover Designer: Alan Furst, Inc.
Cover Photography: Daniel Treat
Illustrator: Ken Jacobson
Production Manager: Peggy Naylor

ISBN 0-7644-2545-5
10 9 8 7 6   12 11 10 09 08 07

Printed in the United States of America.

How to Let the Lord Build Your House
and not labor in vain

●

The HomeBuilders Parenting Series®: A small-group
Bible study dedicated to making your family all that God
intended.

FamilyLife is a division of Campus Crusade for Christ
International, an evangelical Christian organization founded in
1951 by Bill Bright. FamilyLife was started in 1976 to help
fulfill the Great Commission by strengthening marriages and
families and then equipping them to go to the world with the
gospel of Jesus Christ. The Weekend to Remember conference
is held in most major cities throughout the United States and is
one of the fastest-growing marriage conferences in America
today. "FamilyLife Today," a daily radio program hosted by
Dennis Rainey, is heard on hundreds of stations across the
country. Information on all resources offered by FamilyLife may
be obtained by contacting us at the address, telephone number,
or World Wide Web site listed below.

Bringing Timeless Principles Home

Dennis Rainey, Executive Director
FamilyLife
P.O. Box 8220
Little Rock, AR 72221-8220
1-800-FL-TODAY
www.familylife.com

A division of Campus Crusade for Christ International
Bill Bright, Founder
Steve Douglass, President

About the Sessions

Each session in this study is composed of the following categories: Warm-Up, Blueprints, Wrap-Up, and HomeBuilders Project. A description of each of these categories follows:

Warm-Up (15 minutes)

 The purpose of Warm-Up is to help people unwind from a busy day and get to know each other better. Typically the first point in Warm-Up is an exercise that is meant to be fun while introducing the topic of the session. The ability to share in fun with others is important in building relationships. Another component of Warm-Up is the Project Report (except in Session One), which is designed to provide accountability for the HomeBuilders Project that is to be completed by couples between sessions.

Blueprints (60 minutes)

 This is the heart of the study. In this part of each session, people answer questions related to the topic of study and look to God's Word for understanding. Some of the questions are to be answered by couples, in subgroups, or in the group at large. There are notes in the margin or instructions within a question that designate these groupings.

Wrap-Up (15 minutes)

This category serves to "bring home the point" and wind down a session in an appropriate fashion.

HomeBuilders Project (60 minutes)

This project is the unique application step in a HomeBuilders study. Before leaving a meeting, couples are encouraged to "Make a Date" to do the project for the session prior to the next meeting. Most HomeBuilders Projects contain three sections: (1) As a Couple—a brief exercise designed to get the date started; (2) Individually—a section of questions for husbands and wives to answer separately; and (3) Interact as a Couple—an opportunity for couples to share their answers with each other and to make application in their lives.

Another feature you will find in this course is a section of Parent-Child Interactions. There is a corresponding interaction for each session. These interactions provide parents an excellent opportunity to communicate with their children on the important topics covered in this course.

In addition to the above regular features, occasional activities are labeled "For Extra Impact." These are activities that generally provide a more active or visual way to make a particular point. Be mindful that people within a group have different learning styles. While most of what is presented is verbal, a visual or active exercise now and then helps engage more of the senses and appeals to people who learn best by seeing, touching, and doing.

About the Authors

Dennis Rainey is the executive director and the co-founder of FamilyLife (a division of Campus Crusade for Christ) and a graduate of Dallas Theological Seminary. Since 1976, he has overseen the rapid growth of FamilyLife's conferences and resources. He began the HomeBuilders Couples Series and the HomeBuilders Parenting Series and is also the daily host of the nationally syndicated radio program "FamilyLife Today."

Dennis and his wife, Barbara, have spoken at FamilyLife conferences across the United States and overseas. Dennis is also a speaker for Promise Keepers. He has testified on family issues before Congress and has appeared on numerous radio and television programs.

Dennis and Barbara have co-authored several books, including *Building Your Mate's Self-Esteem* (re-released as *The New Building Your Mate's Self-Esteem*), *Moments Together for Couples*, *Parenting Today's Adolescent*, and *Starting Your Marriage Right*.

Dennis and Barbara have served on the staff of Campus Crusade since 1971. They have six children and a growing number of grandchildren. They are both graduates of the University of Arkansas and live near Little Rock, Arkansas.

Contents

Acknowledgments

It is appropriate that we thank our children—Ashley, Benjamin, Samuel, Rebecca, Deborah, and Laura—for putting up with imperfect parents who have attempted to apply biblical principles to the art of parenting. We have no greater joy than to know that our children are walking in the truth (3 John 4).

There are great men and women who I work with here at FamilyLife. One of them is Dave Boehi—he is not only a gifted writer, but also a man with a huge heart for the world. Dave you have been The Man when it comes to creating HomeBuilders studies. Your life has touched hundreds of thousands of lives around the world. Thank you for rolling up your sleeves on this HomeBuilders study and for being a pioneer and a great editor. This series would never have happened without you.

Ken Tuttle is another unsung hero in the battle for the family. Ken you have been instrumental in taking these studies and moving them from the book shelf to the hearts of homes in more than 35 countries around the world. Thanks for your faithful leadership that you have given HomeBuilders. You've only begun to fight!

Mike Pickle was a great help in putting this study together. And to the team that keeps me going—Clark Hollingsworth, Janet Logan, Michele English and John Majors: Thanks for the lives you have served and who are forever changed because you cared. Thanks for your faithfulness and hard work!

A special word of thanks to Matt Lockhart, our editor at Group Publishing, for his continued partnership over the last few years with both the HomeBuilders Couples Series and the HomeBuilders Parenting Series. Matt has led many of the studies himself, and provides a high level of expertise in helping us craft these studies.

Introduction

Nearly all of the important jobs in our culture require intensive training. We would not think of allowing someone to practice medicine, for example, without first attending medical school and completing his or her residency.

But do you realize that most people receive little training in how to fulfill one of the most important responsibilities of our lives—being effective parents? When we bring a new life into the world, we burst with pride and joy...but are often ignorant of how to actually raise that child to become a mature, responsible adult.

In response to the need we see in families today, FamilyLife and Group Publishing have developed a series of small-group studies called the HomeBuilders Parenting Series. These studies focus on raising children and are written so that parents of children of all ages will benefit.

For these HomeBuilders studies, we have several goals in mind: First, *we want to encourage you in the process of child rearing*. We feel that being a mom and a dad is a high calling and an incredible privilege. We also know how easy it is to feel overwhelmed by the responsibility, especially when you have young children. Participating in a HomeBuilders group can connect you with other parents who share your struggles. The help and encouragement you receive from them will be invaluable.

Second, *we want to help you develop a practical, biblical plan for parenting*. It's so easy for parents to take parenting one day at a time. But as we've raised our six children, we've learned that we need to understand biblical guidelines on parenting and then make proactive plans on how we will apply them.

Third, *we want to enhance and strengthen your teamwork as a couple*. You will learn together how to apply key biblical truths, and in the HomeBuilders Projects you will talk through how to apply them to your unique family situation. In the process, you will have the opportunity to discuss issues that you may have ignored or avoided in the past. And you'll spend time regularly in prayer, asking God for his direction and power.

Fourth, *we want to help you connect with other parents so you can encourage and help one another.* You could complete this study with just your spouse, but we strongly urge you to either form or join a group of couples studying this material. You will find that the questions in each study will help create a special environment of warmth, encouragement, and fellowship as you meet together to study how to build the type of home you desire. You will have the opportunity to talk with other parents to learn some new ideas...or to get their advice...or just to see that others are going through the same experiences. Participating in a HomeBuilders group could be one of the highlights of your life.

Finally, *we want to help you strengthen your relationship with God.* Not only does our loving Father provide biblical principles for parenting, but our relationship with him allows us to rely on his strength and wisdom. In fact, it is when we feel most power-less and inadequate as parents that he is most real to us. God loves to help the helpless parent.

The Bible: Blueprints for Building Your Family

You will notice as you proceed through this study that the Bible is used frequently as the final authority on issues of life, marriage, and parenting. Although written thousands of years ago, this Book still speaks clearly and powerfully about the struggles we face in our families. The Bible is God's Word—his blueprint for building a God-honoring home and for dealing with the practical issues of living.

We encourage you to have a Bible with you for each session. For this series we use the New International Version as our primary reference. Another excellent translation is the New American Standard Bible.

A Special Word to Single Parents

Although the primary audience for this study is married couples, we recognize that single parents will benefit greatly from the experience. If you are a single parent, you will find that some of the language and material does not apply directly to you. But most of what you will find in this study is timeless wisdom taken directly from Scripture and can help you develop a solid, workable plan for your family. We hope you will be flexible and adapt the material to your specific situation.

If possible, you might want to attend the group sessions with another single parent. This will allow you to encourage each other and hold each other accountable to complete the HomeBuilders Projects.

Ground Rules

Each group is designed to be enjoyable and informative— and non-threatening. Three simple ground rules will help ensure that everyone feels comfortable and gets the most out of the experience.

1. Don't share anything that would embarrass your spouse or violate the trust of your children.

2. You may pass on any question you don't want to answer.

3. If possible, plan to complete the HomeBuilders Project as a couple between group sessions.

A Few Quick Notes About Leading a HomeBuilders Group

1. Leading a group is much easier than you may think! A group leader in a HomeBuilders session is really a "facilitator." As a facilitator, your goal is simply to guide the group through the discussion questions. You don't need to teach the material—in fact, we don't want you to! The special dynamic of a HomeBuilders group is that couples teach themselves.

2. This material is designed to be used in a home study, but it also can be adapted for use in a Sunday school environment. (See pages 135-136—"In a Sunday school class"—for more information about this option.)

3. We have included a section of Leaders Notes in the back of this book. Be sure to read through these notes before leading a session; they will help you prepare.

4. For more material on leading a HomeBuilders group, get a copy of the *HomeBuilders Leader Guide* by Drew and Kit Coons. This book is an excellent resource that provides helpful guidelines on how to start a study, how to keep discussion moving, and much more.

What Every Parent Needs

In today's culture, parents need to establish a strong foundation for their home.

W A R M • U P   15   M I N U T E S

My Name Is...and I'm a Parent

Introduce yourself, and tell the group the names and ages of your children and one reason why you came to this group.

Next choose one of the following sentences to complete, and then share your sentence with the group.

- One way my life definitely changed when I became a parent is...
- One of the best things about being a parent is...
- The longer I'm a parent, the more I appreciate how my own parents (or father/mother)...
- I didn't realize that when I became a parent my life would...

Getting Connected

Pass your books around the room, and have everyone write in names, phone numbers, and e-mail addresses.

_____
NAME, PHONE, AND E-MAIL

_____
NAME, PHONE, AND E-MAIL

_____
NAME, PHONE, AND E-MAIL

_____
NAME, PHONE, AND E-MAIL

_____
NAME, PHONE, AND E-MAIL

_____
NAME, PHONE, AND E-MAIL

BLUEPRINTS   **6 0 MINUTES**

The Challenge of Raising Children Today

There are no perfect people and no perfect parents. All parents face challenges as they raise their children.

1. How would you compare your job as a parent today to what your parents faced? Do you think parenting today is more difficult, less difficult, or about the same?

If you have a large group, form smaller groups of about six people to answer the Blueprints questions. Unless otherwise noted, answer the questions in your sub-group. Before moving on to the Wrap-Up section, have subgroups report to the whole group the highlights from their discussion.

2. Take a couple of minutes to review the chart on the following page, which details some of the changes we've seen in our culture during the last several decades. In what specific ways do you think these changes have created additional challenges for parents?

	1950s	Today
Home Life	big portion of leisure time spent doing things together with family; TV just starting to come into homes children spent time at home; played in neighborhood after school	big portion of leisure time spent with entertainment—TV, video games, computer, music, and Internet—often alone many suburban kids hurried and pressured by a myriad of activities; urban kids often bored, restless
Marriage	marriages more stable; more two-parent homes	increasing number of children growing up in broken homes
Primary Influences	home church school peer pressure: local media: films	home media: TV, films, music, Internet peer pressure: local and national (through media) school
Extended Family	parents often raised family in same town or state where they grew up grandparents, other relatives lived nearby, involved in helping with children	increased mobility leads more parents to raise family in other states more children see relatives infrequently
Culture	values and morals based on biblical truth; "do what is right" school, community, media reinforced values taught at home	relative standards; no absolute truth; "do what's right for me" parents who teach absolute standards are undermined in culture and in some schools media bombards children with multitude of ideas and images many parents fearful of culture's influence on their children
Child Rearing	most mothers at home help from extended family	increasing priority of career over motherhood increasing reliance on day care increasing lack of extended family involvement

The Need for Commitment

As a parent in today's culture, it's easy to feel apprehensive and, at times, inadequate. Our goal in this study is to provide you with some clear principles and strategies to improve your parenting skills. And we'll start by discussing a few foundational needs of any parent today.

3. How strong of a connection do you feel there is between the strength of your marriage commitment and the well-being of your children?

4. In what ways can having and raising children expose weaknesses in a marriage relationship? If you can, give an example.

5. A united approach to parenting requires participation from both parents. What are the benefits to a family when both parents are involved and in agreement in the parenting process? What are some practical day-to-day examples of this approach in action that come to mind?

HomeBuilders Principle:
Parents need a fresh commitment to their marriage and to a united approach to raising their children.

The Need to Value Children

6. Read Psalm 127:3-5 and Luke 18:15-17. What do these passages tell us about God's view of children?

7. In society today, what would you say are typical attitudes—both positive and negative—that parents tend to have toward children?

8. Why do you think it's important for us to acknowledge that each child is a gift—an assignment—from God? How does this view affect your responsibilities as a parent?

9. What are some specific ways your children have been gifts or blessings for you? What's rewarding to you as a parent?

HomeBuilders Principle:
*Each child is a divinely placed gift, a high and holy
privilege given to us as parents.*

The Need for Convictions

One of the most important things we can do as parents is to establish a set of convictions and ideals to live by. One of the best definitions we've found for *conviction* is from author Josh McDowell. Having a conviction, he writes, "is being so thoroughly convinced that something is absolutely true that you take a stand for it regardless of the consequences." These convictions—we also call them "core values"—guide our daily choices and help us establish priorities. They are also the values we pass on to our children.

For example, a statement such as "If you're going to do a job, do it right the first time" is actually a reflection of multiple core convictions: the values of working hard, taking responsibility, and striving for excellence.

10. As you think about your mother and father (or the person who raised you), what really mattered to them—what convictions or values would you say governed their lives? What core values did they pass on to you?

11. On the scale that follows, where would you rate yourself on how well you have determined a personal set of core values or convictions?

Answer question 11 with your spouse. After answering, you may want to share an appropriate insight or discovery with the group.

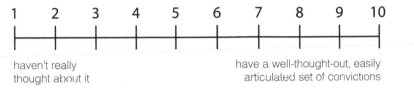

1   2   3   4   5   6   7   8   9   10

haven't really
thought about it

have a well-thought-out, easily
articulated set of convictions

• List a couple of your key convictions or core values:

12. Read Matthew 7:24-27. According to this passage, what's the difference between the wise man and the foolish man? How would you apply this to the process of determining your core values?

HomeBuilders Principle:
Parents today need to establish their core values, and they should base those core values on the unchanging truth of God's Word.

Core Values

Look through the following list, and discuss why it's important to hold some clear convictions in these areas. Then with each couple selecting one or more of these areas, write a sample conviction for the area you picked, and share it with the group. For this exercise, try and keep your sample convictions to one sentence. For example, for the area of "Lifestyle," a sample conviction could be "We'll eat dinner together as a family at least five times a week."

- ***Spiritual:*** importance of establishing a relationship with God and obeying God's commands

- ***Relational:*** how you treat other people

- ***Moral:*** how you determine what's right and wrong

- ***Civic and Cultural:*** your responsibilities to our nation and society

- **Lifestyle:** how you spend your time, what you consider important, your work ethic

- **Family:** commitment to spouse, children, parents, relatives

- **Personal Development:** intellectual growth, health

- **Character:** personal qualities you feel are important to develop

Make a Date

Make a date with your spouse to complete the HomeBuilders Project for this session prior to the next group meeting. Your leader will ask at the next session for you to share one thing from this experience.

_____
DATE

_____
TIME

_____
LOCATION

As a Couple [10 minutes]

To start this project, take turns telling each other about

- the first time you remember one of your deeply held personal convictions being really put to the test. What happened? What did you do?

Individually [20 minutes]

1. Thinking back over this first group session of the study, what was the main thing you got out of this session?

2. What are some steps you can take in order to develop a more united, team approach to parenting?

Determining Your Core Values

3. In the space that follows, or on a separate sheet of paper if you need more room to write, take five to ten minutes to list as many values as you can think of that you would like to pass on to your children. This is brainstorming time: Focus on writing as many convictions as come to mind. To help you get started, look over the list of "Core Values Possibilities" starting on page 28.

4. Working from the list you just created, select five core values to designate as your top values, and record them here:

1.

2.

3.

4.

5.

5. Reflect on your lifestyle and how you spend your time. How well does your life reflect the top core values you selected? Be specific.

Interact as a Couple [30 minutes]

1. Share your answers from the individual section. Be open, kind, and understanding.

2. Talk about the top core values you selected. How similar or different are your lists? Do you agree or disagree with each other's selections? Create a consolidated "Top Ten Core Values" list.

1.

2.

3.

4.

5.

6.

7.

8.

9.

10.

3. Discuss how you can teach and model these values to your children. You might want to get out your calendars and schedule a series of family nights to address your top-ten values with your children.

4. Close in prayer. Ask God for wisdom as you seek to model and communicate your core values to your children.

Be sure to check out the related Parent-Child Interaction on page 115.

Core Values Possibilities

While not an exhaustive list, here are over fifty topics in eight categories to help spark your thinking.

Spiritual Values

Values under this category might address topics like

- a personal relationship with God through Christ
- a childlike faith
- a biblical worldview
- an implicit trust in the Bible
- a contrite and tender heart
- an attitude of humble prayer
- a hunger for righteousness
- a healthy fear and reverence for God
- a radical dependence on God
- a forgiving spirit
- a spirit of hope
- a deep and abiding love for God and others
- a submissive attitude toward God and God-appointed authorities

Relational Values

Values under this category might deal with attitudes like

- respectful
- friendly
- compassionate
- gracious
- merciful
- caring
- thoughtful
- kind
- helpful
- giving
- generous

Moral Values

Values under this category might address topics like

- what you base your moral choices on
- where you stand on specific issues

Civic and Cultural Values

Values under this category might address topics like

- abiding by the law
- social-mindedness
- patriotism

Lifestyle Values

Values under this category might address topics like

- how you spend your time each day
- emphasis on material things
- work ethic
- emphasis on relationships

Family Values

Values under this category might address topics like

- commitment to your spouse
- importance of commitment to each other as a family
- importance of grandparents and relatives

Personal Development Values

Values under this category might address topics like

- personal health convictions
- intellectual growth
- skill and hobby development
- cleanliness
- discipline

Character Values

Values under this category might address traits like

- honesty
- lovingkindness
- truthfulness
- faithfulness
- trustworthiness
- obedience
- teachability
- tolerance
- temperance
- patience
- loyalty
- moral purity
- financial integrity

Building a Relationship With Your Children

Our success as parents hinges on developing a positive relationship with our children.

W A R M • U P   15   M I N U T E S

Memory Makers

Building a relationship with your children involves making memories. Pick one of the following questions to answer and share with the group:

- If you could choose one favorite childhood memory of something you did with a parent, what would it be, and why?
- What's a favorite memory of something you have done with your own children?
- Why is it important to build a storehouse of shared memories with your children?

Project Report

Share one thing you learned from last session's HomeBuilders Project.

BLUEPRINTS   60 MINUTES

The focus in Session One was on establishing a strong foundation for your home. In this session we will look at the type of relationship you need with your children to become a more effective parent.

Expressing Love in a Relationship

A positive relationship with your children is grounded in their knowledge that you love them unconditionally.

If you have a large group, form smaller groups of about six people to answer the Blueprints questions. Unless otherwise noted, answer the questions in your subgroup. Before moving into the Wrap-Up section, have subgroups report to the whole group the highlights from their discussions.

1. Practically speaking, what are some ways you can demonstrate unconditional love to your children when
• they disobey you?

- they don't meet a performance expectation you have clearly set for them (such as cleaning their rooms or completing chores)?

2. Why is it important to show affection for your children no matter what their ages?

Building a Relationship Requires Involvement

3. One of the best places in the Bible to read about the responsibilities of a parent is in the book of Proverbs. Looking at the passages that follow, how would you describe the relationship between the father and son in these verses? What type of parental involvement do you see in regard to the father?

- Proverbs 1:8-10

- Proverbs 3:1-7

• Proverbs 4:1-4

4. What are some of the pressures we face as parents that can make it difficult for us to be vitally involved in teaching, training, and guiding our children?

5. Many parents are very involved in the lives of their children when they are young, but that involvement often decreases as the children approach and enter adolescence. Why do you think this is? Why is continued involvement vitally important?

Answer questions 6 and 7 with your spouse. After answering, you may want to share an appropriate insight or discovery with the group.

6. What are areas of special interest your children have? What are some practical ways you can share with them in their interests?

7. What do you think your children need most from you right now?

HomeBuilders Principle:
Building a relationship with your children requires a commitment to being vitally involved in teaching, training, and guiding them in God's ways.

Building a Relationship Requires Praise

8. Read Proverbs 12:25 and Ephesians 4:29. In what ways can a parent's praise benefit a child?

9. Which seems to come more naturally as a parent—praise or criticism? Why? What are ways parents can intentionally be more lavish with praise and less critical?

HomeBuilders Principle:
One of your children's greatest needs is your praise and approval.

Building a Relationship Requires Resolving Conflict

10. Read Ephesians 6:4. What are some ways parents can exasperate their children? What effect does conflict between you and your child have on the atmosphere in your home?

11. Read Ephesians 4:32. What principles do you find in this verse that are important to model to your children? What are some ways these principles can be practically modeled?

Rules and Relationship in Balance

Children come into the world with the need for both love and guidance.

12. What can happen in a home when

- a parent emphasizes rules and discipline for a child without a complementary warm and loving relationship?

- a parent emphasizes a loving relationship but is light on rules and discipline for a child?

Relationship Building Ideas

As a group, take some time to brainstorm a list of simple, low cost, relationship building activities you can do with your children. You might consider breaking into subgroups, with each group working on a separate list. For example, one group might list activities for young children, while another lists activities for father and son or mother and daughter. Record your ideas in the following space:

After compiling your ideas, review them, and select one or two activities to do with your children in the coming week. Talk with your spouse about how you can help and encourage each other in doing the activities you selected.

Make a Date

Make a date with your spouse to meet before the next session to complete this session's HomeBuilders Project. Your leader will ask at the next session for you to share one aspect of this experience.

_____
DATE

_____
TIMF

_____
LOCATION

Parting Thought

Just as God pursues a relationship with us, we should love our children and pursue a relationship with them. This relationship is like a bridge to an island. The bridge allows traffic to flow in both directions—it allows you to love and encourage your children while training them and building their character. Don't let the bridge go down!

As a Couple [10 minutes]

A good measure of a relationship is how much you know about another person. To evaluate how you're doing in your relationship with your children, answer the following questions. (Answer these questions individually, and then compare answers with your spouse.)

· If you have more than one child, record an answer for each of your children.

- What's your child's favorite song or music group?

- What's a special subject your child has recently studied in school or Sunday school?

- What's your child's favorite game to play?

• Who's your child's best friend?

• What's your child's favorite food?

• What's your child's favorite book?

To see how you did, plan to ask your children these questions later. For now, compare your answers with your spouse, and then discuss these questions:

• How confident are you that you answered most of the questions correctly?

• How close or in touch do you feel with your children right now?

Individually [20 minutes]

1. Look back over this session. What was one way you were challenged?

Reflecting on the Past

2. What did your mother and father do best as they raised you? (If you were raised primarily by someone other than your parents, answer this question with that person in mind.)

Mom	*Dad*

3. What could your parents have done better?

Mom	*Dad*

4. What words would you use to describe your relationship with each of your parents?

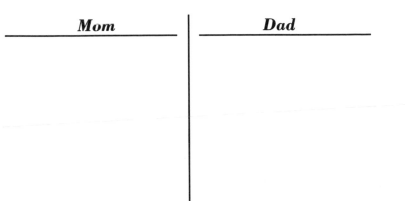

Mom	*Dad*

Reflecting on Today

5. Read Psalm 127:3-5. In what ways has your life been "blessed" by your children?

6. What general observations would you make about your relationship with your children? How well do you think you have truly received your children as gifts from God—accepting them as they are?

7. Now evaluate your relationship with each of your children individually. What would you rate as your top two strengths and needs in each relationship?

	Child:	*Child:*	*Child:*
NEEDS	1. 2.	1. 2.	1. 2.
STRENGTHS	1. 2.	1. 2.	1. 2.

Interact as a Couple [30 minutes]

1. Discuss your answers from the individual section.

2. Decide on two action steps that you would like to begin implementing to improve your relationship with each of your children.

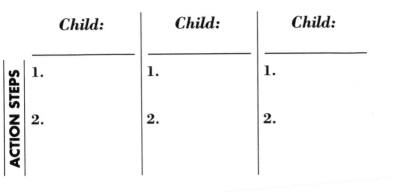

	Child:	Child:	Child:
ACTION STEPS	1.	1.	1.
	2.	2.	2.

3. What's one memory you'd like to make with your child in the next two weeks to build your relationship? (You may want to revisit the ideas from this session's Wrap-Up activity on page 38.)

4. Close in prayer, with each of you completing this sentence: "Dear God, my specific prayer for my relationship with my children is…"

Be sure to check out the related Parent-Child Interaction on page 116.

Dealing With Busyness

The closer you look at your busy schedules, the
more you'll realize how it reflects your values
and convictions.

W A R M • U P   15   M I N U T E S

Busybodies

With the group standing in a circle, follow
these steps:

Step One: Find something to balance on
your plastic utensil, and hold this item steady.

Step Two: While still holding your utensil,
stand on one foot.

Step Three: While holding your utensil and standing on one foot, shake the hand of the person standing closest to you.

Then discuss these questions:

* How would you compare this exercise to the lives
  we try to live in today's culture?

> For this exercise every-
> one will need a plastic
> utensil (preferably a
> knife) and something to
> balance on the utensil—
> a coin, bean, button, or
> potato chip, for example.

- Do you feel busyness is a problem in your family? Explain.

Project Report

Share one thing you learned from last session's HomeBuilders Project.

BLUEPRINTS   6 0   M I N U T E S

Are You Overloaded?

If you have a large group, form smaller groups of about six people to answer the Blueprints questions. Unless otherwise noted, answer the questions in your subgroup. Before moving into the Wrap-Up section, have subgroups report to the whole group the highlights from their discussion.

People throughout history have undoubtedly complained about their busy schedules. But today we have more things than ever competing for our time, our dollars, and our attention—more options, more choices, more entertainment, more noise, more information, more ministry, more volunteer opportunities...more of everything!

1. From the following list, what would you say are the top three factors that contribute the most to a busy schedule for you?

- overcommitment
- job demands
- church involvement
- caring for children
- financial pressures
- unexpected problems
- volunteer responsibilities
- children's extracurricular activities
- health problems
- caring for parents or in-laws
- demands and expectations of extended family
- my own unrealistic expectations
- hobbies and personal interests
- media time (news and entertainment)
- seasonal factors (holidays, school breaks)
- Other:

_____

_____

2. How does your typical weekly schedule—and that of your children—affect you emotionally and physically? How do you think it affects your children?

Two Key Questions

In the first session of this study, we talked about the need for us as parents to develop our core convictions, our core values, and our standards about what is important in life. Dealing with a busy schedule is where the rubber (of our convictions) meets the road (of real life). Why? Because your schedule reflects your values—you devote time to the things that are truly important to you.

To help clarify your convictions and how they relate to your schedule, it's important to ask two questions:

Question One: Why are we doing what we're doing?

3. Why do you think there are so many parents who spend so much time taking their children from one activity (sports practices and games, music lessons, dance, and tae kwon do, to name a few) to another?

4. Another activity that takes up more time than we realize is entertainment—and it's important for us to ask ourselves why. How much extra time would open up in your family's schedule if you instituted a weeklong prohibition in your home of television, movies, music, video/computer games, and the Internet? Why does the thought of doing this sound so radical to most of us?

Question Two: Above all else, where do we feel we need to succeed?

5. When you reach the end of your life, how would you measure whether you were successful? Where do you feel you need to succeed above all else?

6. In what ways have you seen your priorities influenced by the things popular culture says are important to do or to have to be "successful"?

Be Careful How You Live

7. Read Ephesians 5:15-17. What do you think "making the most of your time"means (New American Standard Bible)?

8. What are some ways you've found to walk with wisdom and make the most of your time? What kinds of choices have you made to emphasize the top priorities in your schedule?

Relieving the Pressure

The Scriptures offer a number of practical ways to deal with a busy schedule. Here are three:

Take time to rest.

9. Read Exodus 34:21 and Isaiah 58:13-14. Why do you think God placed such importance on a day of rest? If you can, share how you've applied this commandment in your family.

Deny selfish agendas.

10. Read Philippians 2:1-4. How can the principles in this passage be applied to how we use our time?

Make decisions with your spouse about how you use your time.

Answer questions 11 and 12 with your spouse. After answering, you may want to share an appropriate insight or discovery.

Just after Paul's challenge to the Ephesians to make the most of their time, he exhorts them to be "subject to one another in the fear of Christ" (Ephesians 5:21, NASB). One way we've applied this in our marriage is to be accountable to each other with our schedules.

11. What's one thing you'd be willing to give up to allow more time in your schedule?

12. If you could make one change to open up more time in the schedule of your children or your spouse, what would that be?

HomeBuilders Principle:
It's important to schedule regular time with your spouse—such as a weekly date night—to monitor each other's values and priorities as you determine your schedules.

Case Study

Read this case study aloud, and answer the questions that follow.

Lindsey is a twelve-year-old who has competed in gymnastics since she was six. She has steadily improved, and now her coach wants to move her on to an elite team. She would be required to attend workout sessions three days a week from 4 to 8 p.m., and she would travel out of town for several weekend competitions.

Her parents, Greg and Lynn, are concerned about the impact this schedule would have on Lindsey and their family. On one hand, Lindsey loves gymnastics, and they feel an obligation to help her be as good as she can be. It would help build her character. Perhaps, Greg thinks, she might even earn a college scholarship if she keeps improving.

On the other hand, Lindsey has trouble keeping up with her homework and often has to stay up later than her parents wish. They also have three other children with busy agendas. Their oldest daughter is only a year away from leaving home for college, and Greg and Lynn want to preserve as much family time as possible.

- What options do Greg and Lynn have in this situation?

- What would you suggest they do?

Make a Date

Make a date with your spouse to meet before the next session to complete this session's HomeBuilders Project.

DATE

TIME

LOCATION

HOMEBUILDERS PROJECT   6 0   M I N U T E S

As a Couple [10 minutes]

Take turns telling each other what your "dream" day off would look like.

Individually [20 minutes]

1. What did this session reveal to you—good or bad—about your schedules and priorities?

2. How do you rate the level of busyness for each person in your family? List the name of each member of your family along with a rating on a scale of 1 (not busy at all) to 10 (maxed out).

3. In what ways—positive and negative—are your regularly scheduled activities affecting your family? What, if anything, do you need to give up or modify?

4. List the activities each of your children is involved in. Why do you want your child involved in each of these activities?

5. What family activities do you feel are essential in order to build the atmosphere you desire for your home? What type of weekly interaction do you think is critical for your family?

6. As a family, would you say you have enough time each week to rest and to enjoy one another?

7. What changes do you think you should begin making to ensure that your family's schedule reflects the values and priorities that you have?

Interact as a Couple [30 minutes]

1. Review your answers from the individual section.

2. Discuss how your core convictions should help you make future decisions about your schedules and the schedules of your children.

3. Pull out your calendars and begin making the necessary adjustments to your daily, weekly, and annual schedules. Talk about what decisions need to be made now to begin living according to your priorities.

4. End this time with prayer. Ask God for help in making the right decisions about your schedules.

Be sure to check out the related Parent-Child Interaction on page 117.

The Basics of Discipline and Rewards

Children need training in how to make the right responses to authority and to circumstances in life.

WARM • UP   15 MINUTES

Case Study

Have volunteers read the four parts in the following case study, and then have the whole group discuss the questions that follow.

Narrator: 6:30 p.m. Julia walks through the family room and notices that her ten-year-old daughter, Tanya, is on the computer, sending friends messages on the Internet. One of the family rules is that no child can use the Internet (unless it's for schoolwork) until homework is finished for the night.

Julia: Tanya, have you done your homework?

Tanya: I just have a little more. Can't I do it in a little while?

Julia: You know the rules. Do your homework first.

Narrator: 6:40 p.m. Julia passes through the room again and finds Tanya still on the computer.

Julia: Did you hear what I said? Why are you still on the Internet?

Narrator: Tanya quickly leaves the computer and begins working on her homework. At 7:20 p.m. Tanya is back on the computer.

Julia: Have you finished your homework already?

Tanya: I told you I didn't have much left to do.

Julia: OK, you can stay on until 8:00, and then I want you to take a shower and get ready for bed.

Narrator: 8:10 p.m. Julia is in the kitchen and hears the all-too-familiar sound of Tanya and her older brother, Matthew, arguing. Julia hollers from the kitchen.

Julia: What's the problem in there?

Matthew: I need the computer and Tanya won't get off.

Julia: Didn't I tell you to get off at 8:00? I want you in the shower in three minutes or you're in *big* trouble!

Tanya: I didn't know what time it was! I'll get off in a minute—I just need to say goodbye to all my friends.

Narrator: 8:25 p.m. With Julia now in the laundry room, a scuffle breaks out again in the family room.

Tanya: Leave me alone!

Matthew: Mom, Tanya is still on the Internet!

Tanya: Matthew is trying to shove me off the chair!

Julia: YOUNG LADY, IF YOU DON'T GET OFF THAT COM-PUTER *RIGHT NOW*, I'M GOING TO GROUND YOU FROM THE INTERNET FOR A WEEK!

- In what ways can you relate to the problem Julia is having with Tanya? What are some of the problems you have in getting your children to obey the rules in your home?

- What do you think Julia needs to do?

Project Report

Share one thing you learned from last session's HomeBuilders Project.

BLUEPRINTS · 60 MINUTES

The Big Picture

As we look at the subject of disciplining your chil-dren—or more specifically, disciplining and reward-ing your children—it's important to step back and see the big picture: Setting up a system of discipline and rewards should be part of your plan for *building character in your children.*

If you have a large group, form smaller groups of about six people to answer the Blueprints questions. Unless otherwise noted, answer the questions in your subgroup. Before moving into the Wrap-Up section, have subgroups report to the whole group the highlights from their discussion.

As parents, our job is to build character into our children by training them in how to make right responses to authority and to the challenges they'll face in life. Most parents realize their children require training in everyday living skills—things like tying shoes, cleaning up after themselves, and washing dishes. But your children also need training to develop positive character qualities—the ability to choose right from wrong, for example, or to turn away from temptation. As parents, we need to point our children to a relationship with God in which they turn away from their selfish desires and live in obedience to him.

1. When you think of the subject of disciplining your children, what comes to mind?

2. Read Hebrews 12:7-13. What do we learn about discipline from this passage?

3. Since the Bible compares God's discipline to a father's discipline of his children, it's important to note that in addition to disciplining us, God also rewards us for right choices. Read Deuteronomy 30:15-20. What does God promise to those who love God, obey him, and keep his commands?

4. Why do you think it's important for parents to reward their children in addition to disciplining them?

Discipline: A Four Step Process

Step One: Teach and set clear rules and boundaries.

Parents generally set some common rules and boundaries in their home—to keep a child safe, for example, or to help the home function well. But it's also important to set rules and boundaries to develop character traits in a child. For example, if you're training children to be responsible, you might tell them they're required to clean up their rooms a certain number of times each week and then make it clear what will happen if they don't fulfill this responsibility.

5. What are some examples of clear rules or boundaries you could set to teach children of different ages to

• treat other people with respect?

• be honest?

Step Two: Praise and reward positive choices.

6. Read the verses that follow. If you can, tell the group about something that one of your children has done recently—made a right choice, did a job well—that's worthy of praise or reward.

• Proverbs 16:24

• Ephesians 4:29

• 1 Thessalonians 5:11

7. What are some appropriate rewards you have used in your household for good behavior? See how many you can list in two minutes. (Write down the ideas from different group members, and use this list as a reference for the future!)

Step Three: Correct and discipline for poor choices.

8. Choose one of the following scenarios. What could you do in this situation to correct the child and show how to make a right choice?

• Your eight-year-old son is playing one Saturday

afternoon with a neighbor friend. Another friend, Jason, phones him and asks him to come over to his house. Your son accepts the invitation, then tells his neighbor, "It's time for you to go home now. I'm going over to Jason's house to play."

• You give your fourteen-year-old daughter an allowance of twenty dollars a month for spending money. One week into a new month she approaches you and asks for more money because she has already spent the twenty dollars.

9. For some poor choices, children may only require correction from their parents; for other poor choices, children may need discipline. What do the following verses tell us about the benefits of discipline—punishing and reproving children for wrong choices?

• Proverbs 29:15

• Proverbs 29:17

A Special Word About Spanking

While Scripture makes it clear that spanking can be a useful tool of discipline, in our culture it's increasingly characterized as cruel and even abusive. Because some parents have not used this form of discipline wisely, the entire concept of spanking is coming under attack.

We don't believe we should ignore a biblical concept just because some people don't apply it well. But we do recommend that parents agree on some guidelines for spanking:

1. Determine together what attitudes and actions are deserving of physical discipline. Spanking should not be used indiscriminately; it's just one form of discipline to be used in conjunction with other forms. We've used spanking primarily as a discipline for bad choices that reflect serious character issues—disobedience or lying, for example. We define spanking as a "measured amount of pain" administered to a child to break the will but not the spirit.

2. When you determine your child needs to be spanked:

- Do it promptly, but do it in private, not in public.
- Only spank when you're in control—not when you're angry.
- Assure the child of your love.
- When appropriate, explain to the child why he or she is getting a spanking.
- Use an object that will not harm.
- Hold the child while you do the spanking.
- Following the spanking, pray for the child, and assure him or her of your love.

10. What are some forms of discipline that you have used and found effective for children at different ages?

HomeBuilders Principle:
Parents must be committed to a balanced training program—rewarding children for good behavior and disciplining children for wrong choices.

Step Four: Consistency, repetition, and perseverance are required.

Answer question 11 with your spouse. After answering, you may want to share an appropriate insight or discovery with the group.

11. Sometimes children need training in certain areas over and over and over again. What is one area of character development you've been trying to address with your children that will require a commitment to repetitive training? How can you support each other in this?

Scenarios

With your spouse, choose one of the following scenarios to review. Discuss what you would do in this situation and then tell the group.

Scenario 1: For the first three years after your daughter Sarah was born, whenever groceries were needed, either you or your spouse would stay home with Sarah while the other one went to the store. Now you've started taking Sarah with you to the grocery store, and she's been acting terribly. She grabs food off the shelves and screams when you take it away; when you won't buy candy, she drops onto the floor and throws a tantrum. You're getting ready to take her to the store again.

• How would you handle this situation?

Scenario 2: You've divided a number of household chores between your three children. Your ten-year-old son, Ryan, is responsible for pulling the garbage cans out to the curb each Monday night so they can be emptied the next morning by the city's sanitation department. For several weeks he did his job, but for the last two weeks he hasn't. Last week he claimed he forgot, but this morning when you reminded him about his responsibility, he said, "I'm tired of doing all the work. Do I have to do everything around here? Why don't you do it?"

- How would you handle this situation?

Make a Date

Make a date with your spouse to meet before the next session to complete this session's HomeBuilders Project.

_____
DATE

_____
TIME

_____
LOCATION

Parting Thought

Children will behave like children—you can count on it. That's why Galatians 6:9 is such an encouraging promise: "Let us not become weary in doing good, for at the proper time we will reap a harvest if we do not give up." Above all, don't give up!

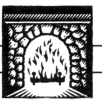

Your goal during this project time will be to develop a plan for how you use discipline and rewards as you build character in your children. At FamilyLife we have talked with scores of parents, and they have repeatedly asked for help in this area.

As a Couple [10 minutes]

Start this project by answering these questions:

- What is the best or most creative reward you ever received? What was it? Why did you get it? How did getting it affect you?

- When is a time you received some form of correction, rebuke, or discipline that stands out in your mind? Did this have a positive or negative effect on you? Explain.

Individually [20 minutes]

1. What insight or concept from this session do you most need to apply in your life or home?

2. How well do you think you use rewards in raising your children? Explain.

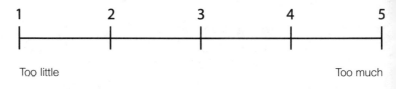

1   2   3   4   5

Too little   Too much

3. Place a check next to the rewards you presently use and a plus sign beside any you would like to implement.

_____ praise and affirmation

_____ hugs and kisses

_____ increased privileges

_____ bonus money

_____ a special activity or trip

_____ a date

_____ a celebration

_____ a valued possession

_____ an award

_____ a special meal

_____ other: _____

4. How do you see yourself as a disciplinarian? Explain.

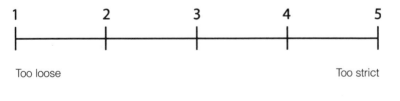

1   2   3   4   5

Too loose   Too strict

5. What do you most appreciate about your spouse in the area of disciplining your children?

6. For the following questions, indicate your level of agreement or disagreement.

I feel my spouse backs me up and doesn't undermine me when I discipline our children.

We are in agreement as a couple about what behaviors we discipline for.

I back up and don't undermine my spouse when he or she disciplines our children.

7. Review the following list, checking the top two or three areas you feel you need to improve in as related to the disciplining of your children.

_____ be more consistent

_____ raise my voice less

_____ be more involved

_____ be more loving

_____ back up my spouse better

_____ reward our children more

_____ be less reactive and more in control

_____ other: _____

8. Is there a particular discipline problem that you need to discuss with your spouse and ask God to help you solve? Explain.

Interact as a Couple [30 minutes]

1. Discuss your answers from the individual time.

2. Agree upon a list of rewards and disciplines that you can use to reinforce what you value. Keep in mind that, to be effective, a discipline needs to either take away something valued or give something not desired. It must also be appropriate for the age of the child.

Rewards	*Disciplines*

Keep this list handy so you can refer to it!

3. Talk through and list the kind of offenses you feel fall under the following categories:

	Major	**Serious**	**Minor**
Younger Children			
Older Children			

Now discuss what type of discipline you feel is appropriate for the different categories of offenses for both younger and older children.

4. Close your time in prayer. Review the items you checked under question 7 from the individual section. Pray for each other about these needs.

Be sure to check out the related Parent-Child Interaction on page 118.

Becoming a Better Parent

Note: For most of this session, you'll be in two groups—one for dads and one for moms, coming back together for the Wrap-Up. The session material for dads starts on this page. For moms, turn to page 88.

Becoming a Better Dad

Fathers need to have a clear, biblical vision of their parental responsibilities.

W A R M • U P   15   M I N U T E S

Talking About Dad

Start this session by discussing these questions:

- When you think of your dad, what words come to mind?

- What's something you learned from your father?

Project Report

Share one thing you learned from last session's HomeBuilders Project.

BLUEPRINTS   6o MINUTES

Dad as Provider

1. What are some factors that make it difficult to be a father today?

2. Many of our fathers viewed their first responsibility as being the primary provider for the family. How did your father provide for your family as you grew up?

3. Read 1 Timothy 5:8. What are ways our families need us to "provide" for them other than economically?

Dad as Manager

One of the biggest challenges many fathers face is getting involved in the lives of their families. Many find it easy to become passive, and let their wives assume nearly all the responsibilities of running the household.

4. Read 1 Timothy 3:4-5. According to this passage, what's one of the key qualifications for someone aspiring to leadership in the church? Why is this qualification so important?

5. When we think of a manager, we often think first of the workplace. What are some characteristics of a good manager in the workplace?

6. Using the chart below, contrast an involved father versus a passive father in different areas of managing the home. How would the involved or passive father act in each area?

	Involved	Passive
Making decisions about family activities and plans		
Handling and budgeting finances		
Resolving conflict		
Teaching and training children in household responsibilities		
Training children in character development		
Developing and maintaining a system of discipline and rewards		

7. What's one area in which you need to be more active?

HomeBuilders Principle:
I'm responsible to God to manage my family well.

Dad as Teacher

8. Looking at the verses that follow, what roles is the father in these passages assuming with his children? As a dad, what are some practical ways you have tried to do the same?

• Proverbs 4:1-5

• Proverbs 4:10-14

• Proverbs 4:20-27

9. As the family minister, you can compare your role to that of a shepherd guiding his flock. Read Psalm 23. In what ways could you apply the duties of a shepherd to your role as a father?

Shepherd	Father
"He makes me lie down in green pastures, he leads me beside quiet waters" (verse 2).	
"He guides me in paths of righteousness" (verse 3).	
"Even though I walk through the valley of the shadow of death, I will fear no evil, for you are with me" (verse 4).	

HomeBuilders Principle:
I'm responsible to serve my family as a minister, seeing that their needs are being met and leading them to seek and serve the Lord.

Dad as Model

10. Read Psalm 101. What kind of person does this psalm call us to be?

11. Why is it important to personally model the values in Psalm 101 as you seek to build them into your children?

12. Read Ephesians 6:4. How can failing to model what you teach exasperate or provoke your children? What else that you do or don't do can be a source of exasperation?

HomeBuilders Principle:
I'm responsible to be a model of Christ to my family. In doing that, I need to live a life of God-honoring character.

Note: For this session's Wrap-Up, turn to page 93.

Becoming a Better Mom

Mothers need to have a clear, biblical vision of their parental responsibilities.

W A R M • U P   15 M I N U T E S

Talking About Mom

Start this session by discussing these questions:

- What kind of influence did your mother have on the person you are today?

- What's something you enjoyed doing with your mom? If you could keep just one memory of you and your mother, what would it be, and why?

Project Report

Share one thing you learned from last session's HomeBuilders Project.

Mom as Home Builder

1. What are the biggest challenges you face in your responsibilities as a mother?

2. In what ways do you feel your upbringing influences your feelings and values about your role as a mom?

3. What do the following Scriptures tell us about the importance and priority of your role as a mother?

• Proverbs 14:1

• Proverbs 31:10-31

• Titus 2:3-5

4. What unique needs does a mom fill in the lives of her children?

HomeBuilders Principle:
Motherhood is a gift of God and an opportunity to impact future generations.

Mom as Nurturer of Children

5. As we read in Titus 2:4, older women are told to encourage younger women to love their children. Why do you think this admonition is given?

6. Why do you think a child needs a mother's love so much? How do you as a mother uniquely nurture your children?

7. What are ways moms can show love to their children? For three minutes, brainstorm as many ideas as you can.

8. What do you think are the consequences children face when they're not loved or aren't sure of their mother's unconditional love?

HomeBuilders Principle:
I'm responsible to love my children so they can see the love of God in and through me.

Mom as Trainer of Children

9. Read Proverbs 22:6. How does a mother uniquely train her children?

10. What types of things do your children need training in right now?

11. If you can, tell the group about an area in which you think you did or are doing a good job of training your children. Share what you did or are doing.

12. As you look at your own children, what do you think are the greatest needs to address in their lives right now?

HomeBuilders Principle:
I have a responsibility to prepare the next generation to shoulder the responsibilities of husband and wife, father and mother.

W R A P • U P   15 M I N U T E S

Remember Me

This session started with dads remembering their fathers and moms remembering their mothers. With your spouse, discuss the following question:

Note: For the Wrap-Up, the groups of dads and moms should be together.

• What do you want to be remembered for by your children?

If comfortable doing so, relate your answers to the group.

Make a Date

Make a date with your spouse to meet before the next session to complete this session's HomeBuilders Project.

_____
DATE

_____
TIME

_____
LOCATION

Parting Thought

One of the greatest needs in our nation is for men and women to stand up and be the fathers and mothers our children need and the Bible instructs us to be. We need to be there when they are young children, teenagers, career singles, married husbands and wives, and parents. Your job and responsibility never ends. I challenge you to step up to the responsibilities God has for you in your family.

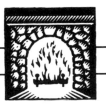

As a Couple [10 minutes]

Start this project by answering these questions:

- What stands out in your mind as something your parents did right in raising you?

- What's one thing you especially appreciate about your spouse as a parent?

Individually [20 minutes]

Dads and moms: There are separate questions 1-3 for you to answer. Then prior to coming back together, answer questions 4-6.

Questions for Dads

1. Look back over the material you and the other men discussed during the group session. What points had the most impact on you and why?

2. In the group session, the involved father was contrasted with the passive father. Rate your level of involvement with your children in the following areas:

	Passive/not involved				Actively involved
Making decisions about family activities and plans	1	2	3	4	5
Handling and budgeting finances	1	2	3	4	5
Resolving conflict	1	2	3	4	5
Teaching and training children in household responsibilities	1	2	3	4	5
Training children in character development	1	2	3	4	5
Developing and maintaining a system of discipline and rewards	1	2	3	4	5

3. If you could choose just one improvement you could make as a dad, what would that be and why?

Questions for Moms

1. Look back over the material you and the other women discussed during the group session. What points had the most impact on you and why?

2. In the group session, two responsibilities of mothers were discussed: loving their children and training their children. How do you feel you are doing in these areas? Explain.

3. If you could choose just one improvement you could make as a mom, what would that be and why?

Questions for Dads and Moms

4. What's one thing you feel you do well in your role as a parent?

5. What's one way you can be more supportive of your spouse in the role of parent? Be specific.

6. Is there anything you feel you should be doing as parents that you're not currently doing? If yes, explain.

Interact as a Couple [30 minutes]

1. Tell each other the main things you learned during the split-group session.

2. Share with each other your answers to the questions in the individual section of this HomeBuilders Project.

3. Read Proverbs 22:6. Talk about any specific areas of training your children especially need right now and what you can or should do as a mom or dad to provide this training.

4. Finish your time in prayer, asking God to give you the strength and power to follow through on any commitments you make to become an even more effective father or mother.

Be sure to check out the related Parent-Child Interaction on page 119.

Building a Firm Foundation

The most important step to improving your parenting is bringing God into your family.

W A R M • U P   15   M I N U T E S

Sand Castles

Back in Session One we looked briefly at Matthew 7:24-27, where Jesus talks of wise and foolish builders. Now let's look at this passage one more time in a way that will make it come to life. Follow these steps, and then discuss the questions that follow. *Note: This is an exercise you can use to teach the same lesson to your children!*

For this exercise you'll need
- a rock, approximately the size of a softball,
- two or three cups of sand,
- a pitcher of water, and
- a large metal, glass, or foil pan (a 9x13 cake pan or larger).

Step 1: Put the sand in the pan, and then pour a little water on to it, just enough to make the sand wet enough so that you can mold it into shapes. Have one or two people form a small sand castle on one side of the pan. When they're finished, place the rock on the other side of the pan.

Step 2: Read aloud Matthew 7:24-27. Then have someone pour the pitcher of water over the sand castle and the rock. Then discuss these questions:

- What can we learn from this exercise? Write down your observations, and then share them with the group.

- Why is a spiritual foundation like the one described in Matthew 7:24-27 necessary for your family?

Project Report

Share one thing you learned from last session's HomeBuilders Project.

Battling the Storms

1. In Matthew 7:24-27, what do you think the rain, floods, and wind symbolize for us today?

If you have a large group, form smaller groups of about six people to answer the Blueprints questions. Unless otherwise noted, answer the questions in your sub-group. Before moving into the Wrap-Up section, have subgroups report to the whole group the highlights from their discussion.

2. What kinds of "storms" have hit your family recently?

3. If you can, tell the group about a time when you experienced firsthand the truth of this passage—a time when your trust in God and his Word gave you the strength to withstand a storm in your life.

4. Different types of storms occur during the different seasons. As you look toward the next few years, what storms do you envision hitting your family?

HomeBuilders Principle:
For your family to withstand the storms of life, you need to build a foundation rooted in God and his Word.

Hearing and Obeying the Word

Over the course of this study on improving your parenting, we've discussed many practical principles of parenting that are taken from the Bible. In doing so you've had the opportunity to hear God's Word and apply it to your life. This practice (Bible study *with* life application) and prayer are two of the most basic, but essential components of a spiritual foundation for your family.

5. Read James 1:22-25. Why do you think both hearing and doing are necessary to build a spiritual foundation in your home? Which is more difficult and why?

6. Read 2 Timothy 3:14-17. What does this passage tell us about the value of Scripture? What's one way Scripture has been useful to you or to your family?

7. With your spouse, read the following passages from Christ's Sermon on the Mount.
- Matthew 5:38-46
- Matthew 6:25-34

Then as a couple, discuss the following questions:
- Think about a time you've applied the truth of one of these passages in your family and with what result?

- What truth from these passages does your family most need to apply right now, and why?

Then, if comfortable doing so, share with the group your response to one of the above questions.

Talking With God

God has given us an incredible privilege—the ability to converse with him. Praying daily with your spouse and with your children will help you grow closer to God and to each other.

8. With each couple taking one or more of the following passages, read your verses with your spouse, and discuss what the verses tell you about prayer. Then report to the group a summary of your verses and insights.

- Psalm 34:15-18
- Jeremiah 33:3
- Matthew 7:7-11
- Romans 8:26-27, 34b
- Philippians 4:6-7
- 1 Thessalonians 5:17
- 1 John 5:14-15

9. Which do you find easier, praying alone, praying together as a family, praying with your children, or praying with your spouse? Why?

10. In what ways have you experienced the benefits of prayer—as an individual, as a couple, or as a family? If you can, share with the group some things you have done that have helped you to pray together as a couple or as a family.

11. How can this group best pray for you? What needs are in your life that require God's intervention? (Before moving into Wrap-Up, spend a few minutes praying for the requests that were shared.)

HomeBuilders Principle:
Through Bible study and prayer, we have the opportunity to build a relationship with God.

Building on the Rock

Ultimately the most important aspect of building a strong spiritual foundation for your family is you and your relationship with God. God wants a personal relationship with you and has made this relationship possible through Jesus Christ.

You could say each of us, whether we realize it or not, walks through life on a type of spiritual journey—a personal quest to learn what's important, what's true…to find God. Different individuals are at different points on this journey:

- Some people have never taken time to seriously consider the truth of Scripture and the claims of Christ.
- Others are seeking for truth, yet haven't come to a decision about whether to commit their lives to Christ.
- Some believe they're Christians but then look closely at their lives and realize that they really don't have a personal relationship with Christ.
- Some have committed their lives to Christ but struggle with a type of "roller-coaster" experience;

they go through times of walking closely with Christ and times of spiritual dryness.

- Finally, others have made a personal commitment to Christ and have learned to walk consistently in trust and obedience to God.

Individually review these questions and record your responses. Then relate to the group whatever you would like to share.

- On your spiritual journey, where would you say you are? Do any of these descriptions apply to you, or would you state them in a different way?

- In what ways has participating in this group affected your view of God and your need for a relationship with him?

Make a Date

Make a date with your spouse to meet in the next week to complete the final HomeBuilders Project of this study.

_____
DATE

_____
TIME

_____
LOCATION

Parting Thought

Many parents reach a point where they realize something is missing in their family life—a spiritual foundation. They realize they need God in their family and in their lives, but they don't know what to do. Often it takes a storm of life to reveal this need.

If you have questions about whether you have personally established a relationship with God, we suggest reading the article "Our Problems, God's Answers" (p. 124) and talking to your HomeBuilders leader about what it means to be a Christian.

HOMEBUILDERS PROJECT   6 0   M I N U T E S

As a Couple [10 minutes]

Congratulations—you've made it to the last project of this study! Start your date by reflecting on what impact this course has had on you by discussing these questions:

- What has been the best part of this study for you?
- How has this study benefited your marriage?
- In what ways has this course helped you as a parent?

• What is something new you have learned or discovered about your spouse? yourself? your children?

Individually [20 minutes]

1. What was the most important insight or lesson for you from this session?

2. Overall, what has been the most important insight or lesson for you from this course?

3. Looking back, what's one step or action—something you want to do, stop doing, or change—that you identified during this course and that you need to follow up on? What needs to happen for this to become a reality?

4. What have been some of the major storms your family has weathered so far? How have you seen God at work in your family during the hard times?

5. How would you rate your family's past efforts in building a spiritual foundation? On the scale that follows, circle how you would rate yourself, then put a box on your rating for you and your spouse together, and then an X on your rating for your efforts as a family.

	Poor				Good
Prayer	1	2	3	4	5
Bible study	1	2	3	4	5

6. Practically, what is one thing you could do individually to improve the rating you gave yourself in the areas of prayer and Bible study? What steps could you take as a couple or family to better practice these spiritual disciplines together?

7. Look again at this session's Wrap-Up (p. 108). Write down a few thoughts about where you are on your spiritual journey so that you can share them with your spouse.

If you're unsure whether you're a Christian or are frustrated with your spiritual life, be sure to read the special article "Our Problems, God's Answers" (p. 124). It will give you insight into how to become a Christian and also how to walk with Christ on a daily basis.

Interact as a Couple [30 minutes]

1. Share your answers from the individual section with your spouse.

2. Decide together on two or three action points for strengthening the spiritual foundation of your family. Here are some suggestions:

• Commit to spending time with God daily in Bible study and prayer.

• Commit to praying daily with each other. This has been the most important commitment we've made together as a couple.

• Commit to organizing family devotions every week or two. If you haven't done the Parent-Child Interactions yet (p. 115), that's a great place to start.

3. Evaluate what you can or should do or continue to do to strengthen your home. You may want to consider continuing the practice of setting aside time for date nights. You may also want to review the list of ideas on page 123.

4. Spend a few minutes in prayer together. Thank God for each other and for your children. Pray for God's wisdom, direction, and blessing as you continue to seek to improve your parenting and strengthen the spiritual foundation of your family.

Be sure to check out the related Parent-Child Interactions on page 120.

Please visit our Web site at www.familylife.com/homebuilders to give us your feedback on this study and to get information on other FamilyLife resources and conferences.

Parent-Child Interactions

Interaction 1
Family Values

This activity provides the opportunity for you to tell your children about your "core values"—the convictions you and your spouse hold and consider to be the most important. Make sure you complete the Session One HomeBuilders Project before you begin this interaction with your children.

1. Ask your family, "What do you think are some of the values we think are most important for us to live by? What things are true, no matter what?"

If you think it's necessary, provide an example by saying, "For instance, here's one: Always tell the truth."

2. Ask, "Where do we get these values from?"

3. Say, "We believe that a home is only as strong as its foundation. Does anyone know what a foundation of a house is?"

If anyone is unsure, take the family outside and show them the foundation of your house (or for the building you live in).

4. Have someone read Matthew 7:24-27. Ask, "What does this passage say about what makes a house strong?"

5. Say, "We believe that a home should be founded on the truth of God's Word. Ultimately, that's what real family values are—truths for living that are based on the Bible."

6. Share a few of the core values you and your spouse discussed during the Session One HomeBuilders Project. If possible, tell the children what Scriptures those values are based on.

Interaction 2
In the Spotlight

In this exercise, you'll direct your family in expressing love and praise for each individual. This is a powerful experience if everyone participates in the right spirit. If you've never done this with your children, it may seem a bit awkward at first. Your children may be hesitant to participate, but with your leadership they will soon get in the spirit.

1. Call the family together at a time when no one will be hurried. Have someone read Proverbs 12:25 and Ephesians 4:29. Then ask, "What do these verses tell us?"

2. Explain that you want your home to be a place where people are loved and encouraged. Say, "We need to love each other unconditionally, and we need to take time to praise each other for right behavior and attitudes. Sometimes, in the midst of living with each other every day, we don't express this often enough. But tonight each person in the family is going to have a chance to be 'in the spotlight' and receive encouragement."

3. Choose someone who will be in the spotlight first. (If you wish, you could use a flashlight and train the light for a few moments on this family member, making a show over being in the spotlight.) Say, "Each person in the family is going to have the chance to be in the spotlight, and during that time all the others are required to say at least two things aloud that they like or appreciate about this person. For example, you could say, 'I like his sense of humor' or 'I appreciate how she always helps me get ready for school each morning.' " Be prepared to get the family started with some comments of your own.

4. When you finish with one person, move to another. Give everyone the chance to be in the spotlight. When you're done, ask, "How did it feel when you were in the spotlight?"

Interaction 3

Busybodies

This project provides a fun demonstration of what it's like to live a hurried life. It's based on the Warm-Up exercise you completed during your group session. Everyone will need a plastic utensil (preferably a knife) and something to balance on the utensil: a coin, bean, button, or potato chip, for example.

1. With your family standing in a circle, follow these steps:
Step 1: Find something to balance on your plastic utensil, and hold this item steady.

Step 2: While still holding your utensil, stand on one foot.

Step 3: While holding your utensil and standing on one foot, shake the hand of the person standing closest to you.

2. Then discuss these questions:

- How did you feel trying to accomplish all those things at the same time?

- Are there times when you think you're trying to do too many things?

- Do you feel busyness is a problem in our family? Explain.

3. Read Ephesians 5:15-17. Ask, "What do you think 'making the most of your time' means (NASB)?"

4. Ask, "What should be our top priorities—the most important things to keep doing, no matter what?"

5. Ask, "If you could change just one thing to make your schedule easier, what would that be?"

Interaction 4

You Play the Parent!

Building character involves helping your children learn to make right choices. One of the best ways to teach this is by using hypothetical situations like the ones that follow. These two short scenarios (taken from the group session) give your children the chance to not only examine how to make the right choices, but also to think about what it's like to be a parent instead of a child.

1. Tell your children the following story:

You're an adult with an eight-year-old son. He's playing one Saturday afternoon with a neighbor friend. Another friend, Jason, phones him and asks him to come over to his house. Your son accepts the invitation, then tells his neighbor, "It's time for you to go home now. I'm going over to Jason's house to play."

2. Ask, "As the parent, what do you need to tell your son?"

3. Instruct a child to read Galatians 5:14. Then ask these questions:

- What does this passage tell us about how we should treat people?

- What do you think it means to "love your neighbor as yourself"?

4. Now read the next story to your children:

You've divided a number of household chores between your three children. Your ten-year-old son, Ryan, is responsible for pulling the garbage cans out to the curb each Monday night so they can be emptied the next morning by the city's sanitation department. For several weeks he does his job, but for the last two weeks he hasn't. Last week he claimed he forgot, but this morning when you reminded him about his responsibility he said, "I'm tired of doing all the work. Do I have to do everything around here? Why don't you do it?"

5. Ask, "As a parent, what would you do in this situation, and why?"

Date Night

This is one of the most popular ideas we've shared at conferences over the years: Take each of your children out for a date! And don't go on a quick trip for fast food—make this a special day or evening. Take your child to a nicer restaurant, then go to a movie, a sporting event, a shopping mall, or somewhere else you both would enjoy.

Take this opportunity to not only have fun with your children but to also teach them about manners and about how to treat the opposite sex. If possible, a father should go on a date with his daughter and a mother should go with her son.

In order to make this special, take the time to call or write an invitation to your child. If you go to a nice restaurant, dress appropriately. If you're a father taking out a daughter, you might give her a flower. And do your best to remember all the manners you've learned over the years: A man opens a door for a woman; a man pulls the chair out for his date and seats her at the table first.

Sometime during the course of the evening, read aloud Romans 12:10, "Be devoted to one another in brotherly love. Honor one another above yourselves." Then discuss these questions:

- What do you think this verse means?

- How does it apply to the way you treat your brothers or sisters?

- How does it apply to the way a husband and wife should treat each other?

- How do you think this applies to relationships between both boys and girls and men and women?

Interaction 6

Sand Castles

This exercise is the same as the Session Six Warm-Up. It provides a graphic illustration of the type of foundation we need for our homes and serves as a wrap-up for this series of six Parent-Child Interactions. Be sure to complete the other five interactions before doing this one.

For this exercise you'll need

- a rock, approximately the size of a softball,
- two or three cups of sand,
- a pitcher of water, and
- a large metal, glass, or foil pan (a 9x13 cake pan or larger).

1. Divide the following responsibilities among your children, so they can all be involved:
   - Put the sand in the pan.
   - Pour a little water into the pan—just enough to make the sand wet enough so that it can be molded into shapes.
   - Form a small sand castle on one side of the pan.
   - Place the rock on the other side of the pan.

2. Tell one of your children to read aloud Matthew 7:24-27. Then have someone pour the pitcher of water over the sand castle and the rock.

3. Then discuss these questions:
   - What can we learn from this exercise?
   - What's the difference between the foundations that the wise man and the foolish man built?
   - What have we learned over the course of these interactions during the last few weeks about how the Bible helps make each of us stronger?

Where Do You Go From Here?

It is our prayer that you have benefited greatly from this study in the HomeBuilders Parenting Series. We hope that your marriage and home will continue to grow stronger as you both submit your lives to Jesus Christ and build according to his blueprints.

We also hope that you will begin reaching out to strengthen other marriages in your community and local church. Your church needs couples like you who are committed to building Christian marriages. A favorite World War II story illustrates this point very clearly.

The year was 1940. The French Army had just collapsed under Hitler's onslaught. The Dutch had folded, overwhelmed by the Nazi regime. The Belgians had surrendered. And the British Army was trapped on the coast of France in the channel port of Dunkirk.

Two hundred and twenty thousand of Britain's finest young men seemed doomed to die, turning the English Channel red with their blood. The Fuehrer's troops, only miles away in the hills of France, didn't realize how close to victory they actually were.

Any rescue seemed feeble and futile in the time remaining. A "thin" British Navy—"the professionals"—told King George VI that at best they could save 17,000 troops. The House of Commons was warned to prepare for "hard and heavy tidings."

Politicians were paralyzed. The king was powerless. And the Allies could only watch as spectators from a distance. Then as the doom of the British Army seemed imminent, a strange fleet appeared on the horizon of the English Channel—the wildest assortment of boats perhaps ever assembled in history.

Trawlers, tugs, scows, fishing sloops, lifeboats, pleasure craft, smacks and coasters, sailboats, even the London fire-brigade flotilla. *Each ship was manned by civilian volunteers—English fathers sailing to rescue Britain's exhausted, bleeding sons.*

William Manchester writes in his epic book, *The Last Lion*, that even today what happened in 1940 in less than twenty-four hours seems like a miracle—not only were all of the British soldiers rescued, but 118,000 other Allied troops as well.

Today the Christian home is much like those troops at Dunkirk. Pressured, trapped, and demoralized, it needs help. Your help. The Christian community may be much like England—we stand waiting for politicians, professionals, even for our pastors to step in and save the family. But the problem is much larger than all of those combined can solve.

With the highest divorce rate of any nation on earth, we need an all-out effort by men and women who are determined to help rescue the exhausted and wounded casualties of today's families. We need an outreach effort by common couples with faith in an uncommon God.

May we challenge you to invest your lives in others? You have one of the greatest opportunities in history—to help save today's families. By starting a HomeBuilders group, you can join couples around the world who are building and rebuilding hundreds of thousands of homes with a new, solid foundation of a relationship with God.

Will You Join Us in "Touching Lives...Changing Families"?

The following are some practical ways you can make a difference in families today:

1. Gather a group of four to eight couples, and lead them through the six sessions of this HomeBuilders study, *Improving Your Parenting*. (Why not consider challenging others in your church or community to form additional HomeBuilders groups?)

2. Commit to continue building your marriage and home by doing another course in the HomeBuilders Parenting Series or by leading a study in the HomeBuilders Couples Series.

3. An excellent outreach tool is the film *JESUS*, which is available on video. For more information, contact FamilyLife at 1-800-FL-TODAY.

4. Host a dinner party. Invite families from your neighborhood to your home, and as a couple share your faith in Christ.

5. Reach out and share the love of Christ with neighborhood children.

6. If you have attended the Weekend to Remember conference, why not offer to assist your pastor in counseling couples engaged to be married, using the material you received?

For more information about any of the above ministry opportunities, contact your local church, or write:

> **FamilyLife**
> P.O. Box 8220
> Little Rock, AR 72221-8220
> 1-800-FL-TODAY
> **www.familylife.com**

Our Problems, God's Answers

Every couple eventually has to deal with problems in marriage. Communication problems. Parenting issues. Money problems. Difficulties with sexual intimacy. These issues are important to cultivating a strong, loving relationship with your spouse. HomeBuilders Bible studies are designed to help you strengthen your marriage and family in many of these critical areas.

Part One: The Big Problem

One basic problem is at the heart of every other problem in every marriage, and it's a problem we can't help you fix. No matter how hard you try, this is one problem that is too big for you to deal with on your own.

The problem is separation from God. If you want to experience marriage the way it was designed to be, you need a vital relationship with the God who created you and offers you the power to live a life of joy and purpose.

And what separates us from God is one more problem—sin. Most of us have assumed throughout our lives that the term "sin" refers to a list of bad habits that everyone agrees are wrong. We try to deal with our sin problem by working hard to become better people. We read books to learn how to control our anger, or we resolve to stop cheating on our taxes.

But in our hearts, we know our sin problem runs much deeper than a list of bad habits. All of us have rebelled against God. We have ignored him and have decided to run our own lives in a way that makes sense to us. The Bible says that the God who created us wants us to follow his plan for our lives. But because of our sin problem, we think our ideas and plans are better than his.

- *"For all have sinned and fall short of the glory of God"* (Romans 3:23).

What does it mean to "fall short of the glory of God"? It means that none of us has trusted and treasured God the way we should. We have sought to satisfy ourselves with other things and have treated those things as more valuable than God. We have gone our own way. According to the Bible, we have to pay a penalty for our sin. We cannot simply do things the way we choose and hope it will all be OK with God. Following our own plan leads to our destruction.

- *"There is a way that seems right to a man, but in the end it leads to death"* (Proverbs 14:12).

- *"For the wages of sin is death"* (Romans 6:23a).

The penalty for sin is that we are forever separated from God's love. God is holy, and we are sinful. No matter how hard we try, we cannot come up with some plan, like living a good life or even trying to do what the Bible says, and hope that we can avoid the penalty.

God's Solution to Sin

Thankfully, God has a way to solve our dilemma. He became a man through the person of Jesus Christ. He lived a holy life, in perfect obedience to God's plan. He also willingly died on a cross to pay our penalty for sin. Then he proved that he is more powerful than sin or death by rising from the dead. He alone has the power to overrule the penalty for our sin.

- *"Jesus answered, 'I am the way and the truth and the life. No one comes to the Father except through me'"* (John 14:6).

- *"But God demonstrates his own love for us in this: While we were still sinners, Christ died for us"* (Romans 5:8).

- *"Christ died for our sins...he was buried...he was raised on the third day according to the Scriptures...he appeared to Peter, and then to the Twelve. After that, he appeared to more than five hundred"* (1 Corinthians 15:3-6).

- *"For the wages of sin is death, but the gift of God is eternal life in Christ Jesus our Lord"* (Romans 6:23).

The death of Jesus has fixed our sin problem. He has bridged the gap between God and us. He is calling all of us to come to him and to give up our own flawed plan for how to run our lives. He wants us to trust God and his plan.

Accepting God's Solution

If you agree that you are separated from God, he is calling you to confess your sins. All of us have made messes of our lives because we have stubbornly preferred our ideas and plans over his. As a result, we deserve to be cut off from God's love and his care for us. But God has promised that if we will agree that we have rebelled against his plan for us and have messed up our lives, he will forgive us and will fix our sin problem.

- *"Yet to all who received him, to those who believed in his name, he gave the right to become children of God"* (John 1:12).

- *"For it is by grace you have been saved, through faith—and this not from yourselves, it is the gift of*

God—not by works, so that no one can boast" (Ephesians 2:8-9).

When the Bible talks about receiving Christ, it means we acknowledge that we are sinners and that we can't fix the problem ourselves. It means we turn away from our sin. And it means we trust Christ to forgive our sins and to make us the kind of people he wants us to be. It's not enough to just intellectually believe that Christ is the Son of God. We must trust in him and his plan for our lives by faith, as an act of the will.

Are things right between you and God, with him and his plan at the center of your life? Or is life spinning out of control as you seek to make your way on your own?

You can decide today to make a change. You can turn to Christ and allow him to transform your life. All you need to do is to talk to him and tell him what is stirring in your mind and in your heart. If you've never done this before, consider taking the steps listed here:

- Do you agree that you need God? Tell God.

- Have you made a mess of your life by following your own plan? Tell God.

- Do you want God to forgive you? Tell God.

- Do you believe that Jesus' death on the cross and his resurrection from the dead gave him the power to fix your sin problem and to grant you the gift of eternal life? Tell God.

- Are you ready to acknowledge that God's plan for your life is better than any plan you could come up with? Tell God.

- Do you agree that God has the right to be the Lord and master of your life? Tell God.

"Seek the Lord while he may be found;
call on him while he is near"
(Isaiah 55:6).

Following is a suggested prayer:

Lord Jesus, I need you. Thank you for dying on the
cross for my sins. I receive you as my Savior and Lord.
Thank you for forgiving my sins and giving me eternal
life. Make me the kind of person you want me to be.

Does this prayer express the desire of your heart? If it
does, pray it right now, and Christ will come into your life, as
he promised.

Part Two: Living the Christian Life

For a person who is a follower of Christ—a Christian—the
penalty for sin is paid in full. But the effect of sin continues
throughout our lives.

- *"If we claim to be without sin, we deceive ourselves*
  and the truth is not in us" (1 John 1:8).

- *"For what I do is not the good I want to do; no,*
  the evil I do not want to do—this I keep on doing"
  (Romans 7:19).

The effects of sin carry over into our marriages as well.
Even Christians struggle to maintain solid, God-honoring marriages. Most couples eventually realize that they can't do it on
their own. But with God's help, they can succeed. The Holy
Spirit can have a huge impact in the marriages of Christians
who live constantly, moment by moment, under his gracious
direction.

Self-Centered Christians

Many Christians struggle to live the Christian life in their own strength because they are not allowing God to control their lives. Their interests are self-directed, often resulting in failure and frustration.

- *"Brothers, I could not address you as spiritual but as worldly—mere infants in Christ. I gave you milk, not solid food, for you were not yet ready for it. Indeed, you are still not ready. You are still worldly. For since there is jealousy and quarreling among you, are you not worldly? Are you not acting like mere men?"* (1 Corinthians 3:1-3).

The self-centered Christian cannot experience the abundant and fruitful Christian life. Such people trust in their own efforts to live the Christian life: They are either uninformed about—or have forgotten—God's love, forgiveness, and power. This kind of Christian

- has an up-and-down spiritual experience.

- cannot understand himself—he wants to do what is right, but cannot.

- fails to draw upon the power of the Holy Spirit to live the Christian life.

Some or all of the following traits may characterize the Christian who does not fully trust God:

disobedience	plagued by impure thoughts
lack of love for God and others	jealous
	worrisome
inconsistent prayer life	easily discouraged, frustrated
lack of desire for Bible study	critical
legalistic attitude	lack of purpose

Note: The individual who professes to be a Christian but who continues to practice sin should realize that he may not be a Christian at all, according to Ephesians 5:5 and 1 John 2:3; 3:6, 9.

Spirit-Centered Christians

When a Christian puts Christ on the throne of his life, he yields to God's control. This Christian's interests are directed by the Holy Spirit, resulting in harmony with God's plan.

- *"But the fruit of the Spirit is love, joy, peace, patience, kindness, goodness, faithfulness, gentleness and self-control. Against such things there is no law"* (Galatians 5:22-23).

Jesus said:

- *"I have come that they may have life, and have it to the full"* (John 10:10b).

- *"I am the vine; you are the branches. If a man remains in me and I in him, he will bear much fruit; apart from me you can do nothing"* (John 15:5).

- *"But you will receive power when the Holy Spirit comes on you; and you will be my witnesses in Jerusalem, and in all Judea and Samaria, and to the ends of the earth"* (Acts 1:8).

The following traits result naturally from the Holy Spirit's work in our lives:

Christ centered	love
Holy Spirit empowered	joy
motivated to tell others about Jesus	peace
	patience
dedicated to prayer	kindness
student of God's Word	goodness
trusts God	faithfulness
obeys God	gentleness
	self-control

The degree to which these traits appear in a Christian's life and marriage depends upon the extent to which the Christian trusts the Lord with every detail of life, and upon that person's maturity in Christ. One who is only beginning to understand the ministry of the Holy Spirit should not be discouraged if he is not as fruitful as mature Christians who have known and experienced this truth for a longer period of time.

Giving God Control

Jesus promises his followers an abundant and fruitful life as they allow themselves to be directed and empowered by the Holy Spirit. As we give God control of our lives, Christ lives in and through us in the power of the Holy Spirit (John 15).

If you sincerely desire to be directed and empowered by God, you can turn your life over to the control of the Holy Spirit right now (Matthew 5:6; John 7:37-39).

First, confess your sins to God, agreeing with him that you want to turn from any past sinful patterns in your life. Thank God in faith that he has forgiven all of your sins because Christ died for you (Colossians 2:13-15; 1 John 1:9; 2:1-3; Hebrews 10:1-18).

Be sure to offer every area of your life to God (Romans 12:1-2). Consider what areas you might rather keep to yourself, and be sure you're willing to give God control in those areas.

By faith, commit yourself to living according to the Holy Spirit's guidance and power.

- *Live by the Spirit:* **"So I say, live by the Spirit, and you will not gratify the desires of the sinful nature. For the sinful nature desires what is contrary to the Spirit, and the Spirit what is contrary to the sinful nature. They are in conflict with each other, so that you do not do what you want"** (Galatians 5:16-17).

- *Trust in God's promise:* **"This is the confidence we have in approaching God: that if we ask anything according to his will, he hears us. And if we know that he hears us—whatever we ask—we know that we have what we asked of him"** (1 John 5:14-15).

Expressing Your Faith Through Prayer

Prayer is one way of expressing your faith to God. If the prayer that follows expresses your sincere desire, consider praying the prayer or putting the thoughts into your own words:

> *Dear God, I need you. I acknowledge that I have been directing my own life and that, as a result, I have sinned against you. I thank you that you have forgiven my sins through Christ's death on the cross for me. I now invite Christ to take his place on the throne of my life. Take control of my life through the Holy Spirit as you promised you would if I asked in faith. I now thank you for directing my life and for empowering me through the Holy Spirit.*

Walking in the Spirit

If you become aware of an area of your life (an attitude or an action) that is displeasing to God, simply confess your sin, and thank God that he has forgiven your sins on the basis of Christ's death on the cross. Accept God's love and forgiveness by faith, and continue to have fellowship with him.

If you find that you've taken back control of your life through sin—a definite act of disobedience—try this exercise, "Spiritual Breathing," as you give that control back to God.

1. Exhale. Confess your sin. Agree with God that you've sinned against him, and thank him for his forgiveness of it, according to 1 John 1:9 and Hebrews 10:1-25. Remember that confession involves repentance, a determination to change attitudes and actions.

2. Inhale. Surrender control of your life to Christ, inviting the Holy Spirit to once again take charge. Trust that he now directs and empowers you, according to the command of Galatians 5:16-17 and the promise of 1 John 5:14-15. Returning to your faith in God enables you to continue to experience God's love and forgiveness.

Revolutionizing Your Marriage

This new commitment of your life to God will enrich your marriage. Sharing with your spouse what you've committed to is a powerful step in solidifying this commitment. As you exhibit the Holy Spirit's work within you, your spouse may be drawn to make the same commitment you've made. If both of you have given control of your lives to the Holy Spirit, you'll be able to help each other remain true to God, and your marriage may be revolutionized. With God in charge of your lives, life becomes an amazing adventure.

Leaders Notes

Contents

About Leading a HomeBuilders Group

What is the leader's job?

Your role is that of "facilitator"—one who encourages people to think and to discover what Scripture says, who helps group members feel comfortable, and who keeps things moving forward.

What is the best setting and time schedule for this study?

This study is designed as a small-group home Bible study. However, it can be adapted for use in a Sunday school setting as well. Here are some suggestions for using this study in a small group and in a Sunday school class:

In a small group

To create a friendly and comfortable atmosphere, it is recommended that you do this study in a home setting. In many cases, the couple that leads the study also serves as host to the group. Sometimes involving another couple as host is a good idea. Choose the option you believe will work best for your group, taking into account factors such as the number of couples participating and the location.

Each session is designed as a ninety-minute study, but we recommend a two-hour block of time. This will allow you to move through each part of the study at a more relaxed pace. However, be sure to keep in mind one of the cardinal rules of a small group: Good groups start *and* end on time. People's time is valuable, and your group will appreciate your being respectful of this.

In a Sunday school class

There are two important adaptations you need to make if you

want to use this study in a class setting: (1) The material you cover should focus on the content from the Blueprints section of each session. Blueprints is the heart of each session and is designed to last sixty minutes. (2) Most Sunday school classes are taught in a teacher format instead of a small-group format. If this study will be used in a class setting, the class should adapt to a small-group dynamic. This will involve an interactive, discussion-based format and may also require a class to break into multiple smaller groups (we recommend groups of six to eight people).

What is the best size group?

We recommend from four to eight couples (including you and your spouse). If you have more people interested than you think you can accommodate, consider asking someone else to lead a second group. If you have a large group, you are encouraged at various times in the study to break into smaller subgroups. This helps you cover the material in a timely fashion and allows for optimum interaction and participation within the group.

What about refreshments?

Many groups choose to serve refreshments, which help create an environment of fellowship. If you plan on including refreshments in your study, here are a couple of suggestions: (1) For the first session (or two) you should provide the refreshments and then allow the group to be involved by having people sign up to bring them on later dates. (2) Consider starting your group with a short time of informal fellowship and refreshments (fifteen minutes), then move into the study. If couples are late, they miss only the food and don't disrupt the study. You may also want to have refreshments available at the end of your meeting to encourage fellowship, but remember, respect the group members' time by ending the study on schedule and allowing anyone who needs to leave right away the opportunity to do so gracefully.

What about child care?

Groups handle this differently depending on their needs. Here are a couple of options you may want to consider:

- Have group members be responsible for making their own arrangements.
- As a group, hire child care, and have all the kids watched in one location.

What about prayer?

An important part of a small group is prayer. However, as the leader, you need to be sensitive to the level of comfort the people in your group have toward praying in front of others. Never call on people to pray aloud if you don't know if they are comfortable doing this. There are a number of creative approaches you can take, such as modeling prayer, calling for volunteers, and letting people state their prayers in the form of finishing a sentence. A tool that is helpful in a group is a prayer list. You are encouraged to utilize a prayer list, but let it be someone else's ministry to the group. You should lead the prayer time, but allow another couple in the group the opportunity to create, update, and distribute prayer lists.

In closing

An excellent resource that covers leading a HomeBuilders group in greater detail is the *HomeBuilders Leader Guide* by Drew and Kit Coons. This book may be obtained at your local Christian bookstore or by contacting Group Publishing or FamilyLife.

About the
Leaders Notes

The sessions in this study can be easily led without a lot of preparation time. However, accompanying Leaders Notes have been provided to assist you in preparation. The categories within the Leaders Notes are as follows:

Objectives

The purpose of the Objectives is to help focus on the issues that will be presented in each session.

Notes and Tips

This section will relate any general comments about the session. This information should be viewed as ideas, helps, and suggestions. You may want to create a checklist of things you want to be sure to do in each session.

Commentary

Included in this section are notes that relate specifically to Blueprints questions. Not all Blueprints questions in each session will have accompanying commentary notes. Questions with related commentaries are designated by numbers (for example, Blueprints question 2 in Session One would correspond to number 2 in the Commentary section of Session One Leaders Notes).

Session One:
What Every Parent Needs

Objectives

In today's culture, parents need to establish a strong foundation for their home.

In this session, parents will...

- enjoy getting to know one another.
- examine different ways our changing culture has put extra pressure on parents today.
- discuss their need to develop convictions, embrace the value of children, and commit themselves to a team approach to parenting.

Notes and Tips

1. Welcome to the first session of the HomeBuilders course *Improving Your Parenting.* While it's anticipated that most of the participants in this HomeBuilders Couples Series study will be couples with children, be aware that you may have single parents, future parents, or even one parent from a marriage participating. Welcome everyone warmly, and work to create a supportive and encouraging environment.

You'll find certain features throughout this study that are specifically geared toward couples, such as designated couples questions and the HomeBuilders Projects. However, we encourage you as the leader to be flexible and sensitive to your group. For example, if you have a single parent in your group, you might invite that person to join you and your spouse when a couple's question is indicated in the study. Or, if there are multiple single parents, you may want to encourage them to join together for these questions. Likewise, for the HomeBuilders Project at the end of every session, you may want to encourage singles to complete what they can individually or to work with another single parent on the project.

2. If you have not already done so, you will want to read the "About the Sessions" information on pages 4 and 5 as well as "About Leading a HomeBuilders Group" and "About the Leaders Notes" starting on page 138.

3. As part of the first session, you may want to review with the group some Ground Rules (see page 11 in the Introduction).

4. Be sure you have a study guide for each person. You'll also want to have extra Bibles and pens or pencils.

5. Depending on the size of your group, you may spend longer than fifteen minutes on the Warm-Up section. If this happens, try to finish the Blueprints section in forty-five to sixty minutes. It's a good idea to mark the questions in Blueprints that you want to be sure to cover. Encourage couples to look at any questions you don't get to during the session when they do the HomeBuilders Project for this session.

6. You will notice a note in the margin at the start of the Blueprints section that recommends breaking into smaller groups. The reason for this is twofold: (1) to help facilitate discussion and participation by everyone and (2) to help you be able to get through the material in the allotted time.

7. Throughout the sessions in this course, you'll find questions that are designed for spouses to answer together (like question 11 in this session). The purpose of these questions for couples is to foster communication and unity between spouses and to give couples an opportunity to deal with personal issues. While couples are free to share their responses to these questions with the group, be sensitive to

the fact that not all couples will want to do so.

8. With this group just getting underway, it's not too late to invite others to join the group. During Wrap-Up, challenge everyone to think about someone he or she could invite to the next session.

9. Before dismissing, make a special point to tell the group about the importance of the HomeBuilders Project. Encourage couples to "Make a Date" before the next meeting to complete this session's project. Mention that you'll ask about their experience with the project at the next session.

In addition to the HomeBuilders Projects, there are six Parent-Child Interactions (starting on page 115)—one related to each session. These are designed to help give parents an opportunity to communicate with their children. Though we recommend that parents try to complete the interactions between group sessions, we know that this will be a challenge. We encourage couples to place a priority on completing the HomeBuilders Projects and then doing the Parent-Child Interactions when they have time, whether between sessions or at a later date.

10. To conclude this first session, you may want to offer a closing prayer instead of asking others to pray aloud. Many people are uncomfortable praying in front of others, and unless you already know your group well, it may be wise to slowly venture into various methods of prayer.

Commentary

Here's some additional information about various Blueprints questions. The numbers that follow correspond to the Blueprints questions of the same numbers in the session. Be aware, notes are not included for every question. Many of the questions in this study are designed for group members to draw from their own opinions and experiences. If you share any of these points, be sure to do so in a manner that does not stifle discussion by making you the authority with the "real answers." As you share these notes, keep in mind that these sessions are designed around group interaction and participation.

2. Many of the trends we've seen over the last several decades make it more of a challenge to maintain a solid family. One of the biggest problems is that we are now in an adversarial relationship with the culture concerning our children. In the past, biblical values were generally reinforced in popular media, by local communities, and by schools. Now there's an all-out war over values that takes place every day. Children are encouraged to seek out sensual pleasure, affirm materialism, show disrespect for parents, rebel against authority, and regard the belief in absolute standards as an outdated concept.

3. For one thing, it markedly increases your children's sense of security. If your children know that father and mother are fully committed to the marriage and the family, they can focus on growing and maturing rather than worrying about whether mom and dad will split up or whether they caused their parents divorce. Another benefit is that children learn by the parents' example how to love one another, how to love in spite of difficulties, how to handle conflict, and how to persevere through difficulties.

Potential follow up questions: Ask if anyone in the group had parents who divorced when he or she was a child. Then ask, "How did this impact you as a child?"

4. To be effective parents, you need to act as a team. Raising children will reveal unresolved differences in your beliefs and your approach to parenting. For example, if one parent is very lenient in discipline while the other is overly strict, this difference may not surface until they are actually dealing with their children.

5. Children feel loved and secure. They know there are definite limits to their behavior. They also know they can't cause division by appealing to one parent over the other.

Potential follow up question: "What can happen in a family when children see that one parent is more involved in their lives than the other?"

6. Children are gifts, a reward from the Lord. They're to be treasured.

7. On one hand, many parents feel overjoyed and blessed to have children. They consider their children to be the most important people in their lives, and they feel no sacrifice would be too great for them. On the other hand, many couples have difficulty giving up their personal ambitions and affluent lifestyles in order to give their children the time they need or to increase the size of their family. Some see their children as possessions—as things to boast about rather than to love and cherish.

8. It should increase our sense of thankfulness, responsibility, and accountability to God as we raise and train our children. It should also push us to seek God's leadership and guidance in the training process. Realizing that we are accountable to God for how we raise our children should make us more aware of our own spiritual growth and accountability to God.

12. In a confusing world where a multitude of differing values are promoted, it's important to base our convictions upon the truth of God's Word.

Attention HomeBuilders Leaders

Session Two:
Building a Relationship With Your Children

Objectives

Our success as parents hinges on developing a positive relationship with our children.

In this session, parents will...

- acknowledge the important role unconditional love plays in forming positive relationships with their children.
- examine the need for parents to be vitally involved with their children and the pressures that often keep them from this involvement.
- discuss the need for parents to praise their children.
- think about how they can build memories for their families.

Notes and Tips

1. Because this is the second session, your group members have probably warmed up to one another but still may not feel free to be completely open about their relationships. Don't force the issue. Continue to encourage couples to attend and to complete the projects.

2. If new people join the group this session, during Warm-Up ask them to share the names and ages of their children and why they came to this group. Also, give a brief summary of the main points from Session One, and have the group pass around their books to record contact information (page 14).

3. Make sure the arrangements for refreshments (if you're planning to have them) are covered.

4. If your group has decided to use a prayer list, make sure this is covered.

5. If you told the group during the first session that you'd be asking them to share something they learned from the first HomeBuilders Project, be sure to do so. This is an opportunity to establish an environment of accountability. However, be prepared to share a personal example of your own.

6. For the closing prayer in this session, you may want to ask for a volunteer or two to close the group in prayer. Check ahead of time with a couple of people you think might be comfortable praying aloud.

Commentary

1. When your children disobey you, you can show love by controlling your emotions: never venting anger when they disobey you, never disciplining in anger, explaining to them why it's so important for them to learn to obey you and God, and taking time to pray with them before and after any discipline.

Note: The numbers that follow correspond to the Blueprints questions of the same numbers in the session.

When they don't meet a performance standard you've set for them, you can affirm your love for them with your words and by a hug. Take time to listen to them, letting them explain their behavior (even if you don't agree with their explanation). And then explain to them why it's important to be responsible and truthful.

2. There's a lot of wisdom in the bumper-sticker question, "Have you hugged your kid today?" Appropriate expressions of affection—both with words and touch—are important tools to use in communicating unconditional love to your children. Younger children need the unconditional acceptance and love communicated by parental affection. Even as children move into the teen years, it's important for mothers to hug their sons and fathers to hug their daughters. When children receive appropriate parental affection and love, they're less likely to be drawn into unhealthy relationships with someone of the opposite sex.

3. The father shows a desire to impart wisdom and discernment and to protect his son from the consequences of sin. His involvement is demonstrated by taking the initiative to talk to his son. He knows what his son is facing in the world, so he warns and cautions him, begging him to listen to the words of love, experience, and caution. Also he does not appear to adopt a cold, authoritarian tone but instead expresses love and hope.

4. Pressures from work, from other responsibilities, and from personal interests can keep parents from spending adequate time with their children. Attitudes that can hamper their involvement include selfishness, laziness, feelings of inadequacy, a preoccupation with seeking their own happiness and fulfillment, and a willingness to hand over major child-rearing responsibilities to a spouse or to the church.

5. For one thing, it's more difficult to build and maintain a relationship with children as they approach and enter adolescence. As a natural part of the maturing process, they begin to "pull away" emotionally—they want to be with friends more, they're more independent, and they don't want to spend as much time with their parents and siblings. When this happens, some parents pull away themselves and fail to put the same effort into raising their children.

Another problem is the mistaken belief that adolescents are able to begin making their own decisions and don't need parental guidance as much as they once did. This attitude is encouraged by popular media and advertising, which often portrays parents as being old-fashioned and restrictive while teenagers are depicted as being capable of making wise decisions. In addition, some parents may feel awkward guiding their teenage children because of mistakes they made at the same age. In reality, adolescents need parental guidance more than ever as they begin to make and face a number of difficult choices.

8. Children want to please their parents, and their parents' praise is critical to their growth. It's a basic building block of how children view themselves and their world.

9. Many parents find it's easier to criticize their children than to praise them. Part of this is an outgrowth of a parent's role as teacher and trainer; it's often necessary to correct a child when he does something wrong. It often takes a conscious effort for parents to begin praising their children for what they do right. If you have a pattern of overreacting and being critical, then it will take a lot of prayer and mental discipline to break this habit. One way to start is to look for one thing every day that you can praise in each of your children. Look for attitudes, actions, and little things that are praiseworthy, like spending time with a younger brother or sister.

10. This includes things like disciplining in anger, not fulfilling a promise, being overly critical, and being too selfish or busy to spend time with them.

12. Rules and discipline without a positive, loving relationship can wound the spirit of the child. A child might come to the place where he or she feels as if "I can never please, be good enough, or do anything right." Eventually this can lead to rebellion and outright rejection of the parents' values.

A loving relationship without discipline can produce permissiveness or a lack of self-discipline in a child. Children may view this approach as a form of rejection, taking the attitude, "My parents don't really care what happens to me." A parent may be a great friend but a terrible mentor.

Session Three:
Dealing With Busyness

Objectives

The closer you look at your busy schedule, the more you'll realize how it reflects your values and convictions.

In this session, parents will...

- recognize the factors that lead to a hurried lifestyle.
- clarify their convictions about priorities.
- focus on three practical ways to make the most of their time.

Notes and Tips

1. Remember the importance of starting and ending on time.

2. This session's Warm-Up calls for everyone to have a plastic utensil (preferably a table knife) and something to balance on the utensil—a coin, bean, button, or chip, for example. The Warm-Up for this session is more active than the other opening exercises thus far. Have fun with this. The goal of this exercise is simply to get the group to try and do many things at once.

3. As an example to the group, it's important that you and your spouse complete the HomeBuilders Project each session.

4. During Wrap-Up, make a point to encourage couples to use "Make a Date" to complete the HomeBuilders Project for this session.

5. Congratulations! With the completion of this session, you'll be halfway through this study. It's time for a checkup: How's the group going? What has worked well so far? What things might you consider changing as you approach the remaining sessions?

6. You and your spouse may want to consider writing notes of thanks and encouragement to the members of your group this week. Thank them for their commitment and contribution to the group, and let them know that you're praying for them. (Make a point to pray for them as you write their notes.)

Commentary

3. Children do enjoy being involved in these types of activities, but in many cases the parents are pushing the kids into too much involvement. Parents feel pressure to make sure their children are developing athletically, intellectually, or musically so that they will be "successful." Children also need time to rest, play, and be with their families.

Note: The numbers that follow correspond to the Blueprints questions of the same numbers in the session.

4. We have become so accustomed to entertainment—particularly television—that we can hardly imagine a day without it. We also use entertainment as an escape from responsibility and reality. The thought of abstaining from media entertainment for even a brief period seems radical because, for most, it has become an integral part of life.

7. "Making the most of your time" means seeking God's wisdom about our priorities and choices so that we can accomplish what God has for us.

9. God knows how much we need rest. God gave us the command to observe the Sabbath because of this and because, if properly observed, it will lead us closer to him.

10. Philippians 2:1-4 is an appeal to make the needs of others more important than our own needs. At the base of many decisions about time is the natural tendency to do what we desire. If we first deny our own selfish agendas, we can then look for ways to spend our time meeting the needs of our family.

Session Four:

The Basics of Discipline and Rewards

Objectives

Children need training in how to make the right responses to authority and to circumstances in life.

In this session, parents will...

- look at the subject of setting up a system of discipline and rewards as a part of building their children's character.
- work through a four-step process in setting up a plan for disciplining and rewarding their children.
- discuss real-life scenarios for applying these principles.

Notes and Tips

1. Physical discipline is a controversial subject in our culture today. Although this session doesn't examine the subject of spanking closely, it does include the feature "A Special Word About Spanking." You may want to read this feature (p. 69), and then invite comments. If there's disagreement, make two points: (1) We should not ignore what Scripture says, even when we don't totally understand it or agree with it; and (2) physical discipline can be an effective tool for building character in children, as long as it's not abused.

For a more in-depth look at the topic of discipline, the group may have an interest as a potential future study the HomeBuilders Parenting Series course, *Establishing Effective Discipline for Your Children.*

2. By this time, group members should be getting more comfortable with each other. For prayer at the end of this session, you may want to give everyone an opportunity to pray by asking the group to finish a sentence that goes something like this: "Lord, I want to thank you for…" Be sensitive to anyone who may not feel comfortable doing this.

3. You may find it helpful to make some notes right after the meeting to help you evaluate how this session went. Ask yourself questions such as: Did everyone participate? Is there anyone I need to make a special effort to follow up on before the next session?

4. Looking ahead: For the next session, dads and moms will be in separate groups for most of the session. You'll need to have a person lead the group that you're not in. Your spouse may be a good choice for leading the other group. Be sure to make arrangements for this.

Commentary

1. To some people the word *discipline* has negative connotations—they immediately think of spanking or even physical abuse.

Note: The numbers that follow correspond to the Blueprints questions of the same numbers in the session.

2. This passage compares God's relationship with us to that of a loving father's relationship with his child. It implies that disciplining a child is a normal part of that relationship and that this is a positive thing for a child. While discipline is filled with sorrow while it's taking place, it yields "a harvest of righteousness and peace."

4. Rewards are as important a part of parenting as discipline. In addition to correction for wrong choices, children should see and experience the benefits of making right choices.

Session Five:
Becoming a Better Parent

Note: For most of Session Five, dads and moms are in separate groups. Leaders Notes for the moms' group start on page 155.

Becoming a Better Dad

Objectives

Fathers need to have a clear, biblical vision of their parental responsibilities.

In this session, fathers will...

- reflect on their own fathers.
- expand their view of their responsibilities as fathers.
- discuss what it means to be a provider, manager, teacher, and model.

Notes and Tips

1. This is the only session in this course where fathers and mothers are in separate groups. We feel it's important for fathers to consider and discuss their unique responsibilities with other men who face the same challenges.

2. The Warm-Up questions are designed to help dads open up with each other. You might want to tell the men that sometimes it's difficult to talk about our own fathers because of the experiences we've had with them. But sometimes this discussion is necessary if we truly want to become effective fathers ourselves. We don't want our own children to find it difficult to talk about us when they are adults.

3. If your group of dads is over eight people, you may want to form smaller groups of four to seven men to discuss the Blueprints questions. At the end of Blueprints, have subgroups report to the other groups of men the highlights from their discussions.

Commentary

1. Some of the factors making it difficult to be a father include the demands of a career, community and church activities, and personal activities or hobbies. Another challenge is that the roles of men and fathers is often demeaned in today's media. Men are often portrayed as domineering dictators in the family or as buffoons who don't really know what's going on in the lives of their children.

> **Note:** The numbers that follow correspond to the Blueprints questions of the same numbers in the session.

3. Fathers need to provide spiritually for their families by guiding them to a closer knowledge of how to walk with God. They also need to provide emotionally through encouragement, security, and unconditional love.

While we have a responsibility to provide for our families financially, one of the greatest needs in our country is for men to catch a greater vision. As a father, you have an incredible opportunity to help shape the future by helping shape the character of your children.

4. The most tangible way for the church to judge a man's fitness for spiritual leadership in the church is by examining his leadership in the home. Too many men become passive in the home and allow their wives to manage everything. What God wants is for husbands and fathers to be active, engaged, and responsible for their families.

5. They accept the responsibilities assigned to them. They give time. They gain knowledge and understanding of the people entrusted to them. They delegate responsibilities to others well. They know how to train others.

8. He's taking the roles of leader, teacher, and counselor.

9. A father provides rest and refreshment for his family, not only physically but also emotionally and spiritually. A father guides his children to make choices that please God and help them walk with God and grow in their faith. A father protects his children, sometimes physically but often by showing them how to deal with the temptations of life.

11. Children learn as much by the example they see as they do by our instruction. If our actions and our words don't match, our children will know that our words mean very little.

12. If you have more than one version of the Bible in your group, read Ephesians 6:4 from various translations. And encourage dads to give specific examples for this question.

Becoming a Better Mom

Objectives

Mothers need to have a clear, biblical vision of their parental responsibilities.

In this session, mothers will...

- reflect on their own mothers.
- reaffirm the priority of their responsibilities as mothers.
- discuss what it means to be nurturers and trainers of their children.

Notes and Tips

1. This is the only session in this course where fathers and mothers are in separate groups. We feel it's important for mothers to consider and discuss their unique responsibilities with other women who face the same challenges.

2. The Warm-Up questions are designed to help moms open up to each other. You might want to relate that it's sometimes difficult to talk about our own mothers because of the experiences we've had with them. But sometimes this discussion is necessary if we truly want to become effective mothers ourselves. We don't want our own children to find it difficult to talk about us when they're adults.

3. If your group of moms is over eight people, you may want to form smaller groups of four to seven women to discuss the Blueprints questions. At the end of Blueprints, have subgroups report to the other groups of women the highlights from their discussions.

Commentary

Note: The numbers that follow correspond to the Blueprints questions of the same numbers in the session.

3. These passages speak of the importance of a mother placing her home at the top of her priority list. This is a special challenge for many women today who work outside the home because of necessity or the desire to pursue a career.

4. Many mothers find they fill a unique need of their children for nurturing that their husbands cannot meet. This is especially true in the first few years of a child's life.

6. Not receiving a mother's love can affect a child's emotional stability and security as he or she grows up.

Session Six:
Building a Firm Foundation

Objectives

The most important step to improving your parenting is bringing God into your family.

In this session, parents will...

- examine the spiritual foundations of their families to see if they are firm.
- identify two ways to strengthen their spiritual foundations.
- reflect on their own spiritual journeys as they discuss their need for a relationship with God.

Notes and Tips

1. As a part of this last session of this course, you may want to consider having a person or couple share what the study or group has meant to him or her.

2. Be sure to have the supplies you'll need for the Warm-Up in this session: a rock (approximately softball-size), two or three cups of sand, a pitcher of water, and a large pan (a 9x13 cake pan or larger).

3. Question 8 in Blueprints calls for couples to look up different Scripture passages. This approach allows people to simultaneously examine multiple passages. This saves time and gives group members the chance to learn from one another.

4. In this session's Wrap-Up, group members are encouraged to talk about their own "spiritual journeys." This is a great opportunity for you to try and discern where people may stand with God. There may be some individuals who have never understood the gospel and don't know what it means to be a Christian. Others may need a better understanding of what it means to walk with Christ on a daily basis. A group experience like this often leads people to examine their spiritual lives and determine how to know God.

Be prepared to explain the gospel in the group if it seems appropriate. Or be available to meet with group members to discuss this topic further if they would like. Read through the article "Our Problems, God's Answers" (starting on p. 124).

5. For Extra Impact: Here's a suggestion for making the closing prayer time of this final session special: Have the group form a prayer circle. Then have each person or couple, if comfortable doing so, take a turn standing or kneeling in the middle of the circle while the group prays specifically for them.

6. While this HomeBuilders study has great value, people are likely to return to previous patterns of living unless they commit to a plan for carrying on the progress that they've made. During this final session of the course, encourage couples to take specific steps beyond this series to continue to build their home. For example, you may want to challenge couples who have developed the habit of a "date night" during this course to continue this practice. You may also want to discuss doing another HomeBuilders study.

7. As a part of this last session, devote time to planning for one more meeting—a party to celebrate the completion of this study!

Commentary

1. The rain, floods, and wind can symbolize the storms of life: a job change or loss, deaths, sickness, financial difficulties, major disappointments, personal failures, a crisis in the life of a child, and divorce.

Note: The numbers that follow correspond to the Blueprints questions of the same numbers in the session.

5. It's more difficult to live out what we've heard because it goes against our sinful nature. In other words, we want to do things our way or in ways that are pleasing or satisfying to us. James is telling us to do things according to the Word and will of God.

10. You might want to be ready to share an experience of your own, just in case people in the group have a difficult time initially answering this question.

11. You may want to offer a prayer for these requests, have group members pray together in small groups, or have a few minutes of silent prayer. If your group normally has a closing prayer time, make this question a part of that time.

Does Your Church Offer Marriage Insurance?

Great marriages don't just happen—husbands and wives need to nurture them. They need to make their marriage relationship a priority.

That's where the HomeBuilders Couples Series® can help! The series consists of interactive 6- to 7-week small group studies that make it easy fo couples to really open up with each other. The result is fun, non-threateni interactions that build stronger Christ-centered relationships between spouses—and with other couples!

Whether you've been married for years or are newly married, this serie: will help you and your spouse discover timeless principles from God's Wor that you can apply to your marriage and make it the best it can be!

The HomeBuilders Leader Guide gives you all the information and encouragement you need to start and lead a dynamic HomeBuilders small group.

The HomeBuilders Couples Series includes these life-changing studies:

- Building Teamwork in Your Marriage
- Building Your Marriage (*also available in Spanish!*)
- Building Your Mate's Self-Esteem
- Growing Together in Christ
- Improving Communication in Your Marriage (*also available in Spanish!*)
- Making Your Remarriage Last
- Mastering Money in Your Marriage
- Overcoming Stress in Your Marriage
- Resolving Conflict in Your Marriage

And check out the HomeBuilders Parenting Series!

- Building Character in Your Children
- Establishing Effective Discipline for Your Children
- Guiding Your Teenagers
- Helping Your Children Know Go(
- Improving Your Parenting
- Raising Children of Faith

Look for the **HomeBuilders Couples Series and HomeBuilders Parenting Series** at your favorite Christian supplier or write:

FAMILYLIFE™
Bringing Timeless Principles Home

www.familylife.com

publishing, inc.®

P.O. Box 485, Loveland, CO 80539-0485.
www.grouppublishing.com